Even In Guilford

Shadows on 'The Covenant'

COVENANT

We whose names are hereunder written, intending by God's gracious permission to plant ourselves in New England, and if it may be, in the southerly part about Quinnipiack, we do faithfully promise each to other, for ourselves and our families and those that belong to us, that we will, the Lord assisting us, sit down and join ourselves together in one entire plantation and to be helpful each to other in any common work, according to every man's ability and as need shall require, and we promise not to desert or leave each other of this plantation, but with the consent of the rest, or the greater part of the company who have entered into this engagement. As for our gathering together in a church way and the choice of officers and members to be joined together in that way, we do refer ourselves until such time as it shall please God to settle us in our plantation. In witness whereof we have subscribed our hands this first day of June 1639.

Robert Kitchell
John Bishop
Francis Bushnell
William Chittenden
William Leete
Thomas Jones
John Jordan
William Stone

John Stone
William Plane
Richard Guttridge
John Housegoe
William Dudley
John Permewly
John Mepham
Thomas Norton

Francis Chatfield
William Halle
Thomas Naish
Henry Kingnorth
Henry Dowdy
Thomas Cooke
Henry Whitfield

GREG KINSELLA

EVEN IN GUILFORD
Shadows on 'The Covenant'

Print ISBN: 978-1-66789-492-8
eBook ISBN: 978-1-66789-493-5

CONTENTS

CHAPTER ONE

IN THE LAND OF STEADY HABITS

Something strange and troubling happened in my town in 2021. Now it's happening again, and it could happen in any town in the country. No, I don't live in Washington, D.C.

I live in Guilford, a quiet and friendly little town on the Connecticut shoreline with maritime and agrarian roots. One of the oldest towns in Connecticut, Guilford has a rich and colorful history to which it clings rather stubbornly. Our 'older' houses tend to be measured not by decades but by centuries. The *Henry Whitfield State Museum* is the oldest house in Connecticut—as well as the oldest stone house in New England—dating back to the year that Guilford was settled in 1639.

My love affair with Guilford was rekindled a few years ago, when treatment for lymphoma (now well-controlled with a daily regimen of medication) conspired with COVID-19 to force a sabbatical from daily swims at the YMCA. A cranky right knee and balky back had already curtailed my jogging career, so I took up walking for exercise. As I began to walk about town, I quickly came to realize that in the past—while jogging—I had mostly directed my attention forward and down at the sidewalks and road in front of me. I found that walking allowed a better opportunity to 'look around.' I rediscovered the classic beauty of Guilford (where every season is a magical treasure) and the congeniality of its residents. These were things that I'd taken a bit for granted after living for over 3 decades in a town with much to admire.

Ancient stonewalls weave around and through Guilford. Antique houses, monuments and plaques are too plentiful to count. Anachronistic granite mounting blocks and hitching posts can still be spotted near the iconic town green. Guilford boasts of five historic museums (this in a town of fewer than 25,000 people). Not far off our shoreline is *Faulkner's Island*, where a lighthouse—which has been dubbed the 'Eiffel Tower of Long Island Sound'—is a source of special pride. President Thomas Jefferson commissioned it in 1802.

Guilford's founding charter was '*The 1639 Plantation Covenant*,' also known as '*The Guilford Covenant*' (or just '*The Covenant*' to the locals). Its concept was laudable. Those first settlers had promised to remain together, to work together, and to help each other, in order to assure their collective survival—and thereby the survival of the hamlet itself. For most of its long existence, that spirit of partnership has served Guilford well. I've lived in Guilford for well over half of my 66 years. We're not a very diverse town (nearly 90% White) but my wife Cathy and I have found comfort in knowing that Guilford's residents tend to be tolerant, welcoming and kind. We gather on the Green to celebrate accomplishments, to back important causes, or to support grieving families. In short, we gain strength through cooperation and teamwork during good times and bad.

It seems like nearly every resident is an amateur historian of sorts. And with its long shoreline to the south; and hills, lakes and farmland to the north, Guilford has a bit of something for everyone. Guilford openly welcomes visitors—tourism is actually a 'thing' in our little coastal town. Throughout the year, revelers flock to our green or fairgrounds for festivals, fairs, concerts and holiday celebrations. One sunny summer weekend not long ago, my daily walk-about-town took me past a bustling 'New England Taco Fest,' where patrons (and their cars) mostly filled the fairgrounds and parking field. Along my return, I looped past the town green, smiling at the spirited celebrants there enjoying the 'Jewish Festival.'

Guilford also has a long a history of helping 'outsiders' in need. During the 19th Century, the *James Davis, Jr. House* on Goose Lane served as a stop on the Underground Railroad. The famous '*Regicide Cellar*' is a point of particular local pride, it being the site of a much-celebrated display of assisting some (*really*) outsiders who had been in acute need. The large plaque on the side of a gray carriage house on River Street commemorates an event that occurred there in 1661, when William Leete, then the Governor of New Haven County, concealed a couple of rather despairing fellows.

Edward Whalley and William Goffe were two of the English judges who had signed the death warrant for King Charles I. As the history goes, after the Restoration of 1660, these so-called 'Regicide Judges' had fled England. They were seeking refuge in a faraway land known as '*New England*.' They were on the run in Connecticut, desperately trying to evade emissaries of Charles II (understandably, since he'd ordered them beheaded), when Governor Leete at great personal risk provided them with aid and shelter.

These days, a more sanguine ritual often plays out just yards to the north of the 'Regicide Cellar.' Traffic routinely stops along River Street as drivers wait patiently—for the most part—whenever a riverfront gaggle of geese decides to waddle across the roadway to sample the fare on the other side (the side where sheep are often grazing).

First Congregational Church sits at the head of the green. Its original 19th century clock (now on display at the *Henry Whitfield State Museum*) did not have a '*minute hand*,' which today feels symbolic: we still don't like to be rushed. And because history and tradition play such a huge role in our collective identity, Guilford's residents tend to resist being pressured into things. We do most things '*ye olde Yankee way.*' I'm sure generations of Guilford parents have counseled youngsters: '*everything in moderation.*' Even our geography lends itself to moderation. Being a coastal town, the waters of Long Island Sound have moderating effects upon our weather, with summers less hot and winters less cold than our inland neighbors.

In recent years, Guilford residents have mostly shrugged off with indifference the tribalism that has defined the national political carnival. Connecticut is known as 'The Land of Steady Habits,' and Guilford epitomizes that description as well as any town. If one were to research 'Classic New England Town,' you might even find pictures and stories about Guilford. As for local politics, during my years in Guilford, they have always reminded me of sports when I was a kid growing up in nearby North Haven.

When my friends and I were kids, we'd often organize sandlot baseball games (or football, basketball or pond hockey depending on the season). We'd meet up at a local field, court or frozen pond, where we would emulate favorite players from our favored teams. We were mostly fans of teams from either New York or Boston. We wore different hats, and didn't all root for the same teams—but we were still friends, during and after our games. And that's how I always viewed local politics in Guilford. For most of my years in town, politics didn't feel 'tribal.' Lawn signs during election season merely identified whom you supported. They certainly didn't identify the property owner as being an 'enemy.'

Policy disagreements have naturally occurred often enough. Which is of course exactly how democracy works. Ideas are proposed and shared; competing ideas are reviewed, discussed, analyzed and debated. In theory the policies adopted will be beneficial to the town as a whole. If things don't work out to the satisfaction of most of the residents, the redress would occur when the next election rolled around. Occasionally things have gotten a bit messy. But disagreements over policy have not made us disagreeable.

Until very recently, that is.

Beginning around 2021, strident forces began to persistently tug at the seams of Guilford's fabric. Years from now, perhaps 2021 will be remembered not just as the year of an attempted coup in Washington, but also as the year of the 'Guilford Race Riot?' It wasn't the type of riot that you'd see on national news—although some national right-wing media outlets took notice. Nothing was broken; people weren't physically injured. But Guilford's collective moral compass was tested. I would describe what I witnessed in 2021 to be an *intellectual* race riot...in Guilford...mostly by White Christian conservatives. I was forced to confront what seemed to me to be a harsh reality: a small segment of my beloved little town seemed to be intentionally stirring up racial animus. As that notion settled over me, I mused to myself: *Seriously? Has the toxic national craziness actually infected Guilford?*

REGICIDE CELLAR

HERE IN JUNE, 1661
WILLIAM LEETE, THEN
GOVERNOR OF NEW
HAVEN COLONY,
CONCEALED FOR
THREE DAYS WHALLEY
& GOFFE, TWO OF
THE JUDGES WHO
SIGNED THE DEATH
WARRANT OF CHARLES I
OF ENGLAND. THEY
WERE SOUGHT BY
EMISSARIES OF
CHARLES II
WHO AFTER THE
RESTORATION,
ORDERED THE
REGICIDES BEHEADED.

CHAPTER TWO

IS NOT...IS TOO...

My first inkling that something troubling might be afoot came from a good friend who's been involved in local Guilford politics for many years (he's my hero; I have nowhere near the patience for politics). In early 2021, he mentioned to me that there had been some odd goings-on in local political circles. Apparently a handful of folks—potential candidates for the Guilford Board of Education (BOE)—were making noise over Guilford's public school curriculum. I asked him whether it was anything serious? I couldn't imagine how it could be—the BOE had always seemed 'above' politics. His response gave me pause. "It could be. Some of this stuff is pretty out there." He told me to pay attention, while expressing his hope that these folks would tire of instigating a tempest-in-a-teapot and fade away.

That discussion had occurred around the time of the violent January 6th insurrection in Washington, D.C., and it would be fair to say that to the extent my attention focused on politics, it was on issues of more national import. My initial instinct was to mostly 'tune out' what little I'd heard of the sparring between Republican candidates for the BOE. To me, it gave the appearance of a clumsy internecine spat, involving a small, albeit strident fringe of our town Republican Party, that took issue with an aspect of our school curriculum.

Given the right-wing tumult over the school curriculum, in our fairly moderate little town, one might have thought that our schools were on the verge of collapse—but such was not the case. Guilford schools had not been 'circling the drain,' on the brink of demise. Families weren't yanking kids out of our schools at a record pace because of lagging rankings or poor student achievements. To the contrary, for years Guilford's schools have been ranked among the best in the state (and Connecticut schools consistently rank among the best in the country). Guilford schools had an 'A' rating, and were ranked in the *top 4% in the country* by '*Niche*,' a popular school ranking service. In addition to those lofty rankings, Guilford's music, drama, art and athletic programs have been the envy of most towns.

From what I gathered, the most conspicuous issue on the minds of these '*curriculum cops*' was something called 'Critical Race Theory' (CRT). These folks were vigorously, loudly, adamantly opposed to CRT being taught in Guilford schools. Impassioned 'letters'—often from the same people—kept appearing in our local paper (*The Guilford Courier*). Quite frankly, I found the whole squabble fairly bewildering.

I'd have thought that these folks—who apparently *really* hated CRT (whatever the heck that was?)—would have taken great comfort in knowing that CRT was ***not*** part of our school curriculum. The Guilford Public Schools curricula followed all State of Connecticut educational guidelines. At least, so stated every person in a position to know, from our educators and staff, to BOE members, to Superintendent Paul Freedman. A relevant aside: the Connecticut Association of Public School Superintendents named Dr. Freeman the '*2021 Connecticut Superintendent of the Year*.'

Even though everyone in the Guilford public educational system assured us that it was NOT part of the school curriculum, I was still curious: what was this CRT business? Some quick research revealed that it was an advanced academic framework, taught at the college level and beyond, that analyzed and theorized about the lingering structural effects of America's centuries-long history of institutionalized racism.

To get a bead on this brewing squabble in Guilford, I reviewed some recent developments on the educational front. I recalled that there'd been a statewide initiative to acknowledge this nation's long history of legalized racism—a history that included laws that expressly permitted institutions such as slavery and segregation. It would be difficult to find anyone who could seriously dispute those well-documented historical facts.

Along those same lines, in 2021 the Connecticut State Department of Education expressed the goal of "*improving the academic lives of Connecticut's increasingly diverse student body. This includes sustaining equitable and welcoming learning environments in which all students feel valued, respected, and safe to learn and grow...*"

There seemed to be a very broad coalition of educational associations that agreed with that stated goal, as spelled out in a '*Joint Statement on the Importance of a Culturally Responsive Education*' (officially released on July 14, 2021). The following groups had joined in that statement: *Connecticut State Department of Education; Connecticut Association of Public School Superintendents; Connecticut Association of Boards of Education; Connecticut Association of Schools; American Federation of Teachers of Connecticut; Connecticut Education Association.*

That Joint Statement contained the following language:

"We believe and fully support fostering inclusive and culturally responsive educational environments that welcome, respect, and acknowledge the individual identities of all members of a school community as a cornerstone of preparing each and every student to succeed in college, career, and civic life."

It wasn't exactly a radical idea to foster a respectful and welcoming educational environment for all students. Encouraging such an environment would seem a far cry from teaching the curricula contained in college or post-graduate level courses on Critical Race Theory. The 'CRT-in-the-curriculum' theory that was causing all the fuss in Guilford seemed to have been super-charged by a BOE statement that had been issued on April 26, 2021.

That statement, entitled *'Equity and Social Justice in Guilford Public Schools,'* indicated that it had grown out of a long-running debate in Guilford about the Guilford High School 'Indians' mascot, and it was in response to demands for action from over 200 community members, parents and Guilford Public School students, teachers and alumni. The BOE and Dr. Freeman stated their *"commitment to our students and our community to better address instruction and school culture regarding issues of social justice and institutional racism."* That 4/26/2021 statement included the following:

Institutional racism is a part of American history and educators must explicitly address this reality and create a culture that helps eradicate it moving forward. Guilford Public Schools must strive to be a community in which all students feel safe, supported, and recognized, and must support critical thinking about all aspects of our history and current experience. This is done by engaging and supporting students in rigorous exploration of historical and current documents, consideration of a variety of resources, careful analysis of the arguments made and the strength of the evidence supporting them, and classroom discourse. Guilford Public Schools aims to develop critical thinkers and thoughtful citizens. None of our students is responsible for this history, but each will be responsible for their own participation in our local, national, and global communities as they emerge into adulthood.

Some members of our Guilford community have publicly voiced their disagreement with aspects of the school district's social justice initiative, accusing Dr. Freeman of advancing and the Board of Education of supporting an approach to instruction and school culture aimed at indoctrinating students in an ideology that is itself racist. Some have suggested that the school administration has changed school curriculum in support of this aim. Neither of these claims is true. The equity and social justice initiative is not based on any particular ideology, curriculum, or text. The school curricula have not been changed and cannot be changed without public Board of Education approval.

We, members of the Board of Education, are fully supportive of the work addressing equity and social justice within Guilford Public Schools. We support the ongoing curricular audit and the addition of a part-time Equity Liaison and the student teacher Residency Program in the next school year…

As part of the 'Equity and Social Justice' initiative, the BOE reported having heard presentations from faculty about how the Social Studies curriculum was implemented; and from two expert consultants (Dr. Donald Siler of the University of St. Joseph; and Dr. Sharon Locke from Area Cooperative Educational Services), working with students, teachers and leaders in our schools, on an educational approach known as *'culturally responsive teaching.'*

My quick research revealed that 'culturally responsive teaching' referred to an educational approach that strives to use students' customs, characteristics, experience, and perspectives for better classroom instruction. The goal of that approach was to create an environment in which all students feel valued, respected, and safe to learn and grow.

CHAPTER THREE

WHAT THE HECK ARE WE
EVEN TALKING ABOUT?

I was frankly baffled by the loud fringe in Guilford, led by five Republican candidates for the Board of Education, which seemed to vigorously oppose such a learning environment. In summary: (1) Guilford's public school system is among the best in the country; (2) Guilford has the top Public School Superintendent in Connecticut; and (3), everyone involved in the Guilford school system has said that Critical Race Theory was **not** part of the curriculum. Nevertheless, five Republican candidates for the Board of Education, and a cadre of their vocal supporters, stubbornly continued to insist: 'is too.' Also, that CRT is bad…*really bad!*

I began to notice letters in the *Guilford Courier* complaining about controversial books that some of our educators had read during the summer. They seemed most agitated by a book by Ibram X. Kendi entitled *How to Be an Antiracist*. That's right—it was a book that had been read by teachers. It had not been assigned or taught to students as part of the formal curriculum. Okaaay…

These folks seemed to be concerned that using a culturally responsive teaching approach that welcomed, respected and acknowledged the individual identities of all students might somehow be detrimental to White people. I saw the terms '*Marxist*' and '*racist*' bandied about in a few letters published in the *Guilford Courier*. Anyway, that appeared to be the basic foundation of the claim that an advanced academic framework known as 'Critical Race Theory' was actually being taught in Guilford schools as part of its formal curriculum. That complaint seemed to me to conflate an educational method or approach with formal 'curriculum.'

Culturally Responsive Teaching…Equity…Social Justice…Critical Race Theory. Were the 'educational approaches' somehow inseparable from the social science 'theory?' Was it possible that the entire quarrel was a matter of semantics? Was one side defining 'curriculum' differently than the other? The educators and school administrators certainly seemed to have a different understanding of the term 'curriculum' than the five *socially conservative* BOE candidates and their supporters. And of course, the first letters of 'Culturally Responsive Teaching' happened to be 'CRT' (time would tell whether that was mere coincidence). For the typical *Guilford Courier* reader—or at least for me—it had all become a bewildering blizzard of recriminations and denials.

Not surprisingly, a few lawn signs began to pop up around town, promising that these curriculum conspiracy theorists would "*Stop CRT and Politics in our Schools.*" That seemed a rather brazen platform, since they seemed to have created the CRT conspiracy theory in Guilford, and in so doing, had introduced politics into the equation. As they say: 'if it ain't broke? Pretend loudly that it is…and then, promise to fix it.'

I had to concede that if the claims of these folks were actually true, it would be troubling, since that would indicate a vast ongoing conspiracy throughout the school district. The suggestion was that nearly everyone within the school system had been lying to us. If true, the alleged conspiracy was not only vast (the biggest in Guilford history no doubt). It also must have been incredibly successful, because even though these allegations had been circulating for several months, I hadn't seen or heard of any real evidence to support the allegation that our educators, staff members, administrators, BOE members and our Superintendent of Schools had been skillfully lying to us.

By the middle of the summer of 2021—with the curriculum conspiracy theorists searching high and low for the proof—the hundreds of conspirators must have kept quite a tight lid on their scheme. I guess that meant they were incredibly cunning and disciplined? Another explanation, of course—which seemed to me somewhat more likely—was that the alleged conspiracy was more-or-less apocryphal. The conspiracy theorists seemed to be plucking words and phrases like 'racism' and 'critical thinking' and 'social justice' and stirring them all into a grand conspiracy casserole. That would mean the CRT conspiracy cops were the ones conflating and mischaracterizing concepts and facts.

I hoped that wiser heads would prevail, and that our Republican Town Committee would reject the five CRT conspiracy candidates (most of whom seemed to have little experience in education), and would endorse less extreme candidates for their fall primary. The other slate within the Republican caucus included existing Republican BOE members who were up for re-election, and were obviously experienced. Those hopes evaporated at the local GOP caucus in late July 2021, when existing Republican BOE members were ousted. The five CRT conspiracy theorists somehow won over the

Republican Town Committee. *They* would be the approved slate for the school board in its upcoming primary.

Suffice it to say that in my mind—until actual evidence was produced—what was going on seemed like pure silliness. My doctors had advised me to avoid stress, which was why I eventually settled upon a workable personal solution. As seemingly unsupported accusations kept re-appearing in the paper, I decided to stop reading them. I tuned out the noise, because the aggravating claims were driving up my blood pressure. Even though I was retired, I still had an irksome habit of thinking like a lawyer. I vowed to await word of any actual evidence of the big Guilford curriculum conspiracy caper; but I tried to pay less attention to the white noise coming from a handful of folks in my nice little town who seemed more interested in creating controversy. Toward what end, I wasn't quite sure.

I did wonder (perhaps wishfully) whether it was all a misunderstanding over terms and definitions? I had certainly had no idea what 'Critical Race Theory' was when I'd first read about it, and I still had only a vague understanding of it. With every accusation and denial that I'd read, the more confusing it had become. It seemed to me as though the whole town could use a good education on the topic.

My attention was eventually drawn back to the subject in August 2021 by an article in the *Guilford Courier* about an upcoming educational forum on Critical Race Theory that was to be sponsored by our Human Rights Commission (HRC). As I began to read the article, I learned that the HRC had invited retired Superior Court Judge Angela C. Robinson to present a tutorial of sorts on CRT. In addition to her impressive judicial career (20 years on the bench), Judge Robinson was also an eminent academic scholar, author, and educator who taught a law school course, on Critical Race Theory, at Quinnipiac University School of Law in Hamden.

Seeing Judge Robinson's name triggered in me an emotional jolt—a vivid memory of a case that I'd handled before her many years previous. It involved a greedy insurance company behaving badly. I couldn't help but sense a connection to the brewing CRT squabble. Was it possible the CRT conspiracy theorists in Guilford had gotten greedy? After all, to have a chance at being elected in Guilford, candidates just needed to be straight shooters above all else, and stick to issues that mattered to most voters. Mischaracterizing or embellishing stuff? Creating a controversy—about race of all things—didn't seem to me to be a winning strategy in my town. I'd always thought of local politics as the gentle tug-and-pull of competing ideas—not a jackhammer on one side, fueled by facile distortions.

That case that I'd tried before Judge Robinson didn't leave its mark on me because it was big or complex. In fact, I seriously doubted she would even remember the matter. It left its mark on me because it was a small and simple case. Yet she treated it with such patience and full, level attention—it was as though it was the most important legal dispute in New Haven County (which of course it was to my client, and therefore to me at that time). When I first saw her name in the paper, I simply smiled, and thought: *Yes…Judge Robinson is absolutely the perfect person to educate us all.*

That small case that I'd handled, more than 20 years previous, informed what I did next, so forgive me a detour: some brief personal history and then a stroll through the minefield known as personal injury law…which was exactly what led me to Judge Robinson's courtroom in the spring of 2000.

CHAPTER FOUR

MESSIN' WITH
THE WRONG PLAINTIFF

I enrolled in law school in the fall of 1979. By 1999, I was in my 20th year '*in the law*,' and a partner at a mid-sized firm in New Haven, where I handled mostly personal injury litigation on the plaintiff's side. I was well into my second decade of butting heads with insurance companies. I'd become fairly tired of the game. In February 1999, that was where I was in my career as I filed a small personal injury lawsuit in the Meriden Superior Court.

For the record, that case shouldn't have required filing a lawsuit. My client was a delightful young lady. The car accident in which she'd been injured was clearly the fault of the other driver—a young man with a poor driving record and minimal insurance ($20,000). That my client's injury was caused by the accident wasn't disputed. By the time she'd concluded her medical treatment, her case was worth more than the available liability insurance coverage.

My client didn't have additional insurance coverage of her own, to protect against injuries caused by '*underinsured motorists*.' That meant the defendant's $20,000 coverage was likely all that would be available to compensate her. A normal insurance company would have simply paid its policy limits. Unfortunately *Infinity Insurance Company*, of Birmingham, Alabama, had been anything but normal in handling the claim. When it refused to offer up its minimal-limits coverage, I was forced to file a lawsuit against its insured. I assumed that legal 'nudge' would be sufficient to convince *Infinity* to pay up.

I was quite wrong about that.

As I was filing that lawsuit, Angela C. Robinson was about 6 months into her first term as a Superior Court Judge. Although I didn't know Judge Robinson, I knew of her. It would not be hyperbole to describe Angela C. Robinson as a legal superstar. After graduating from Yale Law School, she'd worked for two of Connecticut's most venerated law firms, handling insurance defense matters at the first; and then primarily medical malpractice and other litigation (on the plaintiff's side), at the second.

With a law degree from Yale, and litigation experience at esteemed law firms representing both sides (plaintiff and defense), it wasn't surprising when her name surfaced as a candidate for the bench. What was *extremely* surprising was her age when that honor was bestowed upon her. When Angela C. Robinson became a Superior Court Judge in 1998, she was just 33 years old. In Connecticut's long history, that made her the youngest person ever appointed to the bench.

My little case took its place in the superior court queue, plodding along with countless others. Bringing a lawsuit was one thing. But trying a case before a jury, by definition, included a good degree of risk, which was what usually motivated both sides of a dispute to settle. If any additional 'incentive' in that regard was required as a trial date approached, judges would usually provide it by strongly encouraging (and sometimes strong-arming) parties to settle. Although everyone was entitled to his or her day in court, in reality a very high percentage of cases *had* to settle—it was nearly a mathematical necessity. Otherwise, the system would be overwhelmed by too many cases, atop too few resources.

Infinity seemed fine with that math, as it clung to the compensation that was owed to my client. During the year that the case took to wend through the system, my client even offered to settle for $18,000—which was less than the coverage, and less than her case was worth—just to be done with it. She'd done so because jury trials can be unpredictable, expensive, stressful and time-consuming affairs. With minimal insurance coverage, and absent proof of 'bad faith' by the insurer (more on that subject later), the final recovery would likely be limited to that coverage. That makes going to trial particularly unappealing for plaintiffs in such cases, which is why most of them settle before trial.

Infinity's counter offer was *$9000*! That was about the amount of my client's medical bills. It was the type of offer you'd expect when liability (i.e., who caused the accident?) was seriously in dispute. Disagreements in evaluating cases occur routinely. This should not have been such a case. *Infinity* had conceded that its insured had negligently sideswiped my client's car, forcing it off of the road and into a telephone pole.

Luckily my client's seatbelt had kept her face away from the windshield. But the collision had obviously caused her neck injury. That was so clear that *Infinity* didn't even bother to seek an evaluation of the injury by its own medical expert. It didn't challenge the reasonableness of the medical treatment. In short: *Infinity* owned it. The only question was the value of the claim. In my mind it clearly exceeded the $20,000 policy limits that *Infinity* stubbornly refused to offer. It became pretty clear to me early on that *Infinity* was simply using the inherent pressures, and risks of going to trial, to strong-arm a stingier settlement out of my client. That was a common tactic. But this case presented an unusual dynamic.

It turned out I had the perfect client to stare down an insolent insurance company. I knew she would make an excellent witness before a jury. Her injury was legitimate, and she hadn't over-treated. She was likeable, smart and outgoing. She was cute, funny and competitive—a fine athlete in high school not many years previous. And as I learned during our skirmish with *Infinity*, she was intrepid. She willingly followed my advice. But in the game of 'chicken' that *Infinity* was waging—she was all in. In other words, *Infinity* was messin' with the wrong plaintiff.

Despite its minimal coverage limits, going to trial was not without risk to *Infinity*, since the law assumes that every insurance contract contains an *'implied covenant of good faith and fair dealing.'* If it could be shown that *Infinity* had not acted fairly and in good faith, we could potentially sue *Infinity* under the Connecticut 'direct action statute,' to recover the FULL AMOUNT of any judgment that might be obtained if we were to prevail in a jury trial.

In such an action, a 'policy limits' defense would prove difficult for *Infinity* to sustain. It had repeatedly refused to settle within its coverage limits. In my mind that refusal—and its audacious counter-offer—evidenced bad faith. That's why I sent *Infinity* a 'bad-faith' letter, advising that we intended to try the case, obtain a judgment exceeding the policy limits, and then sue it to collect the full judgment based on its failure to act in good faith. Then I issued a warning to my client, born of a nagging tension that had been taunting me for months.

At the moment there was no pressure on us. As we got close to trial, and called its bluff, *Infinity* would likely relent and offer to pay its policy limits. I warned my client that if she were willing to reject such an offer on the eve of trial, the pressure would shift to us. Then, how smoothly things would play out could very well depend upon the judge assigned to preside over the trial, because judges always want to settle cases.

The system depends upon most cases settling—especially small cases (there are always more pressing matters demanding attention). That meant that eventually, a judge might be leaning hard on *us* to settle for the policy limits. If *we* became viewed as the side standing in the way of a settlement, we could be in for a bumpy ride. I knew from experience. Trying a case before an aggravated judge is not a pleasant undertaking. A lot was going to depend upon our trial judge.

CHAPTER FIVE

THANK YOU, YOUR HONOR

Our case was eventually assigned a date in the spring for jury selection, to be followed by trial. That would be when I'd meet the judge to whom the case was assigned for trial: Angela C. Robinson. I was anxious, because she'd have the power to make things uncomfortable for us. Her background was so impressive. Would she view my little case dismissively? With her extraordinary experience, would she display any arrogance about spending her valuable time overseeing such a small case? I was about to find out.

The lawsuit was a year old when defense counsel and I met with Her Honor for a status conference, to discuss the upcoming trial. Judge Robinson's youthfulness (she was about 8 years my junior) might have been disconcerting, were it not for the fact that she was calm, composed and in control. Her equanimity, and a brief exchange of pleasantries, put me somewhat at ease. She opened her file while looking at defense counsel (a smart and pleasant young attorney), and then at me. She inquired where things stood?

"If I may, your Honor," I said, as I launched into my tale of woe about the vexing route the case had wended. I described *Infinity's* disregard of settlement recommendations from both a pretrial judge, and a court-sponsored mediator. I described our repeated offers to settle within the policy limits, in a case in which the defense had fully conceded liability. I described my delightful young client—who now suffered chronic neck pain and stiffness—and *Infinity's* insulting $9,000 settlement offer (from which my client would 'net' a mere $3,000). Finally I advised that I'd just paid our medical expert's hefty fee, to reserve his time to testify at trial. In other words, we were ready to proceed.

When I stopped prattling, defense counsel advised that *Infinity* didn't think the injury affected my client's life that much—but that it could probably improve its offer somewhat. I jumped back in, to point out that it was a little late for that. After forcing my client to bring suit, *Infinity* had ignored us for more than a year. Having refused to make a good-faith offer—while my client was forced to spend her own time and money—it was brazen to suggest that she should *now* accept what should have been paid long ago.

I held my breath. I'd played this out in my head for weeks. It had the potential to get ugly: '*Okay, so you're saying Infinity has been a jerk…but now it's wised up, and might offer its policy limits? And now you want more than the coverage? Seriously?*' To my great relief, Judge Robinson didn't roll her eyes dismissively. In fact, she barely blinked. Her reply was essentially: 'that's why we have trials. So—how long will the case take to try?' Having girded myself to face intense pressure to settle, I felt a palpable sense of relief that Her Honor was going to allow the system to play out. As with any trial, the outcome was not assured. But at least we'd get a fair chance before a jury, without a frustrated judge hectoring away at me in chambers to settle the case. That was really all a plaintiff could ask.

The trial was fairly short, and probably one of Judge Robinson's simpler matters. There were no complicated legal issues, and very few objections. When it ended, I know I thanked Her Honor. But when the case was well behind me, I recall wishing that I had specifically thanked her for simply allowing the case to proceed, without trying to coerce us into a settlement. In my experience many judges, due to concerns over a backlog of cases, would have pressured me hard to settle before trial. It seems like such a small thing. But after behaving badly for years, to be bailed out by a tunnel-vision judge, would have taught *Infinity* nothing at all. In fact, letting it off the hook might have encouraged future misbehavior. If the system 'playing out' had taught *Infinity* a lesson, then going to trial might have actually saved future judicial resources.

Of course, *Infinity* didn't voluntarily pay. After the verdict and entry of judgment (which was about four times what my client had offered to accept just a couple months earlier), *Infinity* did offer to pay its *policy limits*. It was obviously too late for that. I had to sue under the direct action statute to recover the full amount of the final judgment, based upon its bad-faith failure to settle. Soon after that, *Infinity* agreed to settle—better late than never. I don't recall the exact final amount, but my client was fair. She offered a 'carrot,' and agreed to waive some of the interest that had accrued on the judgment. I thought the jury award had been reasonable (more reasonable than *Infinity* had been in the lead up to trial). So thank you jury, for being fair. And thanks, Your Honor, for being patient and wise.

Other than some routine post-trial motions, I didn't see much of Judge Robinson after that—mainly because, not so long after that case, I took a leave of absence from my firm, in order to pursue some other interests for a while. When I eventually returned to practicing law, it was only on a part-time basis. Judge Robinson, on the other hand, was fully devoted to the law. And not surprisingly, as the years passed, her career continued to soar. She became Chief Administrative Judge for the New Haven Judicial District. After 2 decades, she retired from the bench and returned to private practice. She's affiliated with another prominent firm. She's a published author. And she teaches courses at Quinnipiac University School of Law, including *Evidence*, and also…that course on *Critical Race Theory*. Which finally brings me back to the Guilford political madness of 2021.

What happened next? And by 'next,' I mean after I'd finished reading the *Guilford Courier* article that had caught my attention in August 2021? What happened was that I was rudely startled out of my reverie. I learned from that article that someone had anonymously THREATENED Judge Robinson, and basically warned her to stay away from Guilford. Needless to say, when I read that, I was 'seeing red.' I had trouble making complete sense of the intensity of my reaction to a threat against a judge that I barely knew, and hadn't seen in years. All I can say is that suddenly, the local political absurdity no longer felt harmless.

Somehow this unseemly development in my friendly little town felt unusually personal. I was angry. I was embarrassed. And I distinctly remember this sinking thought: *if something like this is happening in Guilford? Then it could literally happen anywhere.* And that's why I purchased a full-page ad on the back page of the *Guilford Courier* (an undertaking that required me to dip into my wine and beer allowance, which is a big deal).

('Ad' as it appeared on the back of the August 26, 2021 edition of the *Guilford Courier*):

school curriculum. A few residents claim that it is. The 'is not'—'is too' nature of the debate reminded me of my own public school days (circa 2nd grade). With 3 kids of my own who thrived in the Guilford school system, I've always trusted our Board of Ed. to do what's right for our children. That's why I tuned out what seemed to me to be 'noise' from a loud, strident fringe. I now realize that was a mistake. I've always felt that it was enough to simply treat everyone with respect, regardless of how they looked or what they believed. Turns out that's not enough. I was startled out of my moral lassitude upon learning of the anonymous threat against someone that I knew a little and respected a lot. That Anony-mailer does not speak for Guilford. His/her words—having been printed in the paper—should not be allowed to hang out there as though they are true. They are not—of that I'm quite certain.

I only know Judge Robinson professionally (I'm a retired attorney). I tried but one jury case before her, 2 decades ago when she was sitting in Meriden and still fairly new to the bench. It was a small matter that she likely wouldn't remember. But lawyers can learn a lot about a Judge during a weeklong trial. I learned that despite her youthfulness, Judge Robinson was as skilled on the bench as she'd been as a practicing attorney. She was smart, thoughtful, fair and respectful of everyone in the process, from the parties and lawyers to the jurors and court personnel. When I first read that she would be presenting a tutorial of sorts on CRT, I knew we had the right person to educate us on exactly what CRT was (and what it wasn't). Then I was sickened to learn that she'd been threatened.

Judge Robinson is scholarly, she is respectful, and she is Black. It can be fairly surmised that the author of said anonymous email is none of those things. The email included the following analysis: 'Guilford is a community of over 96% Whites; they should be taught to love their race as you expect Blacks to do. You should be working to build up your own race, rather than tearing down the culture of other races.' Unlike Anony-mailer, Her Honor has not torn anyone down. Because Guilford does not have a very diverse population, Anony-mailer assumes that its residents wouldn't welcome a conversation on race with a Black scholar and educator. In the opinion of this writer, there is considerable evidence to the contrary.

Thank You: Guilford Board of Education and Educators. Thank You: Judge Robinson—YOU ARE WELCOME to visit my home anytime (just give us an hour's notice to clean the place up).

THIS PAGE PAID FOR BY: Greg Kinsella: 24 Dunk Rock Rd., Guilford

CHAPTER SIX

WELCOME TO GUILFORD
(SORT OF...)

At a later time, it did occur to me that the coward who had sent that anonymous email to Judge Robinson might not have intended it as an actual 'threat.' Maybe that person *thought* that he/she was stating a fact, and warning Judge Robinson (albeit with a breathtaking lack of respect) that people in Guilford wouldn't welcome her—an esteemed and incredibly accomplished jurist, scholar and educator—because she was Black? If that had been the person's deranged thinking, the fact that a disrespectful soul would deign to portray how the people of Guilford felt was still maddening as hell. I wasn't totally naïve. I knew there were intolerant folks everywhere, including in my town. But I was more than sure that a huge majority of people in Guilford would in fact 'welcome' this legal and academic superstar, who had simply responded to an invitation to advance a discussion, by educating us about CRT.

Knowing very little about Critical Race Theory, part of me wanted to audit Judge Robinson's next class at Quinnipiac University School of Law, and learn everything I could about it. The impatient part of me couldn't wait. I did however tune in to the webinar that was presented by our Human Rights Commission the following week, in which Judge Robinson described the basic history and tenets of CRT (she had politely declined to appear in person before the HRC, after having been threatened). She pointed out to the hundreds of people who tuned in to the forum that she was presenting, in less than an hour, a brief outline of Critical Race Theory. The law school course that she teaches lasts a full semester.

Perhaps most germane to the issue causing the uproar—stirred up by a relative few—concerning the Guilford public school curriculum, was this: Judge Robinson pointed out that CRT was taught, as an undergraduate course, at very few *colleges* in the country; that it was almost exclusively taught at universities as a *graduate level* course. Her Honor patiently answered questions—including some predictably 'loaded questions' submitted by obvious conspiracy campers. In response to one such question, she noted that she disagreed with certain assertions and theories espoused in Ibram Kendi's controversial book.

That one-hour program was helpful and informative at a basic level. The gist of what I got from it was that CRT started with certain underlying facts. One was that race is a 'social construct.' Scientists tell us that biologically, there's only one race of humans: Homo sapiens. Society has chosen to distinguish one group of people from another based upon their 'skin color' (i.e. based upon a purely physical trait that is determined by the amount of melanin contained in the skin).

Another fact that underlies CRT is that laws in the U.S. have evolved, over a very long course of time, to finally become 'facially neutral.' For hundreds of years, starting with the early colonies and continuing until the second half of the 20th century, there existed 'de jure' discrimination (laws that explicitly permitted discrimination based upon skin color). Slavery being the most obvious example, sadly there were many more. After civil rights legislation of the 1960's, and subsequent judicial interpretations of the Constitution and other laws, we can now say that 'de jure' discrimination has been eliminated.

Another underlying fact is that even with laws that are now 'facially neutral,' and even though biologically there is only one 'race,' there continue to be measurable *income, wealth and achievement gaps* in the U.S. between Whites and people of color. CRT explores that incongruity, and theorizes about the extent to which lingering 'built-in' structural inequities extant in laws and institutions created in the past (mostly by powerful White men) play a role.

That was my very basic understanding of CRT, as I sat down to begin writing my ad—which of course was not really an ad…it was more of a plea for sanity and tolerance. I wondered about the far-right fringe that had been pitching the CRT conspiracy theory in Guilford? These were not stupid people. It seemed to me that they must have realized that their assertions were untrue regarding CRT in our school curriculum. I wondered why they were making them?

Were they trying to bait people into defending Critical Race Theory? With that thought in mind, I abandoned any urge to join that battle. It felt as though to do so would have simply distracted from the fact that their argument about our school curriculum seemed to be a fallacy, according to those in the know. I was developing my own thoughts about CRT. But I reasoned that if CRT wasn't part of the Guilford school curriculum, then why even engage in a debate on its merits? That was why I spent my wine and beer money to purchase an ad—as though my words would convince anyone of anything.

I did hope that people in town who had never met, nor even heard of Angela C. Robinson, might start paying attention to what the heck was going on in Guilford (like I had); and then hopefully feel outrage (as I did). I worried about my town, and I respected Judge Robinson too much, to say nothing. And my mind kept drifting back to that small case that I'd tried before her. It was a case that should have settled before suit. It was a case where an insurance company had gotten greedy, and tried to use a structural advantage (provided by an over-burdened court system) to save a few thousand dollars more, when their maximum exposure would only have been $20,000. Their greed ended up costing them $70,000.

I fervently hoped that the CRT conspiracy theorists had also gotten greedy, by biting off more than could be digested by residents of Guilford. I hoped that the seemingly cynical tactic of stoking racial animus would backfire. My mind briefly wandered: how ironic that the acronyms for Critical Race Theory (CRT) and Republican Town Committee (RTC) were so similar. I was pretty sure the CRT conspiracy cops would have spotted a Marxist conspiracy, had the Democrats had such a similar acronym. I digress.

Since the CRT conspiracy theorists would be the endorsed slate running in the GOP primary, I was left to hope the Republican primary voters in town would choose other candidates. That felt like a realistic prospect. My Republican friends and acquaintances would accurately be described as 'traditional' Republicans. They seemed likely to be turned off by the whole contrived race war. Their concerns were mostly with issues such as property taxes…town spending…infrastructure (i.e. the usual stuff).

CHAPTER SEVEN

IF HISTORY IS A BAROMETER...
WE'RE IN TROUBLE

I should state for the record that I'm not a life-long Democrat. I'd spent most of my adult life as a registered Independent voter. The rightward drift of the Republican Party prompted me to register as a Democrat in 2008 so that I could vote for Obama in the Connecticut primary. The rightward *lurch* of the GOP in the past several years has given me no reason to change my affiliation. I'm pretty moderate when it comes to fiscal policy, but I do have the social instincts of a Democrat. I don't personally care what people look like, whom they love, which religion they practice—or whether they practice any religion.

People who are kind and tolerant are welcome to visit my home (please call first though). Others are welcome to stay away. One of the few things that I don't tolerate well is intolerance (which I suppose makes me intolerant in a certain sense). I'm hardly a radical lefty—although presumably some must be convinced I'm a Marxist, for even mentioning 'race' in a newspaper ad or letter. The bottom line for me is this: we're into the 3rd decade of the 21st Century. If the notion of fostering a learning environment in schools that is welcoming, tolerant and sensitive to social and cultural differences is considered by some to be a radically liberal concept...then I guess to them I'm a radical liberal.

I don't buy into the 'culture war' brand of neo-conservatism, which to me feels mostly like a cynical attempt to divide and conquer in quest of power. I tend to be suspicious of things that feel extreme, on either side of the political spectrum. I was quite satisfied with Guilford's last Republican First Selectman (akin to our mayor). I've voted for several Republican candidates over the years—though not much lately, because the Republicans that I've liked in the past were moderates, in the mold of former U.S. Representative Chris Shays. That breed of Republican politician is now mostly extinct in Connecticut as well as the rest of New England (it's been 16 years since Connecticut has sent a Republican to Congress). Nevertheless, I freely acknowledge that neither party has a monopoly on good or bad ideas.

A bad idea coming from the left, in my opinion? The slogan 'Defund the Police.' Obviously we aren't going to do away with police. (Better training, accountability, and different approaches to the myriad mental health matters that regularly confront police would certainly make sense though). A bad idea on the part of certain Republicans in my town? In late July 2021, three of the five CRT conspiracy candidates had appeared on *Fox & Friends*. That was not a wise choice, in my humble opinion. Those BOE candidates—Danielle Scarpellino, Nick Cusano and William Maisano (what the *Fox & Friends* host jokingly referred to as the '*Paesan Panel*')—had celebrated their recent ascension at the Guilford GOP Caucus by making their case on that right-wing show.

Those candidates were perfectly entitled to appear on *Fox & Friends*. But again—Guilford's a pretty moderate New England town with a pragmatic and well-educated electorate. Conservatives, moderates and liberals have peaceably coexisted in Guilford for centuries. The current trend of voters may be somewhat to the left, but our pendulum doesn't swing far from the center. So the appearance of those candidates, on that right-wing show, at that particular moment in time, seemed imprudent to me. The culture wars that are a staple of Republican politics in many parts of the country simply don't resonate in Guilford, Connecticut—a fact that had apparently been lost on the CRT conspiracy squad.

In their on-air interview, the candidates described the evidence to support their CRT conspiracy accusations. It seemed to mostly be the same tired gripe that had been voiced repeatedly from the start: if teachers have read controversial books, they must be teaching CRT as part the curriculum. Of course, the most detested book was Kendi's 'How to Be an Anti-Racist,' which they presumably had read (the CRT conspiracy theorists all seem to know it chapter-and-verse). I wondered why teachers who might have read the book had been transformed into lying racist Marxist conspirators; and yet, the CRT conspiracy cops who'd read it hadn't been so afflicted? (I haven't read the book, so I guess I'm safe for now).

A common proposition from these candidates, and their supporters, seemed to be that discussions of race really have no place in our schools. They do seem to like to invoke Dr. Martin Luther King's 'I Had a Dream' speech. I might hazard a guess that these folks haven't always agreed with all of Dr. King's words and teachings. As if to prove their own 'color-blindness,' it's a savvy tactic to quote the aspirational aspect of his dream: that some day all people will be judged solely by the content of their character, and not by the amount of melanin in their skin.

It is true that those words, when first uttered by Dr. King in front of the Lincoln Memorial in 1963, had a divine quality. It is also a fact that 5 years later, a George Wallace-supporting avowed segregationist, assassinated him. If Dr. King were alive today, he would probably tell us that his dream is far from having been realized. He might offer that—intellectual jujitsu aside—the stubborn refusal by some to even discuss racial disparities in many aspects of modern life, is hardly helping to move us toward that more perfect union about which he dreamed.

The more I heard and read from the CRT conspiracy theorists, the more it struck me that in a different time and place (let's say early 17th century Rome), they might have been among the crowd demanding that Galileo be put on trial. I mean, Copernicus's theory that the earth was not the center of the universe was pretty unpopular from the jump. And then, *Galileo* had the gall to invent a telescope, to prove—Biblical teachings notwithstanding—that Copernicus had been right about the earth revolving around the sun. Presumably to all good conservative Christians of the time, what Galileo did must have seemed like an anti-Christian conspiracy of some sort, intended to undermine unassailable Biblical truths.

Back home in my moderate hometown of Guilford in the 21st century, admittedly I don't get out much. But in 2021, I didn't personally know one person who seemed likely to swallow the CRT conspiracy lure. I couldn't imagine most residents having much of an appetite for race-baiting conspiracies. But to paraphrase one of my favorite retired judges: 'that's why we have elections.'

By the time the Guilford GOP primary approached, I'd abandoned my old strategy of 'tuning out.' I was fully engaged, and wondering what the people of Guilford would think and do as we neared what promised to be a very contentious 'off-year' election. One factor that seriously worried me was this: there would not be any important national, or even statewide offices, being contested in our 2021 election. The main issue on the ballot in Guilford in November 2021 would be to fill the 5 seats that were opening up, due to terms expiring on the 9-seat Board of Education. It was certainly not the most exciting of issues to bring people out to the polls in November.

Using history as a barometer, this would be the type of election where voter turnout in Guilford could be *extremely* low. In the previous off-year election (2019), voter turnout in Guilford was reportedly only around 20%. If that history played out again, it could spell trouble. The devotees who believed (or pretended to believe) the CRT conspiracy claim would definitely show up and vote (zealots tend to do that). As to those people who were unlikely to buy into tortured constructions and unsupported allegations? They might just tune out all that noise, and stay at home during an 'off year' election.

CHAPTER EIGHT

ALARM BELLS RINGING

While the CRT conspiracy theory was being bandied about in the local paper in the summer of 2021, I became aware of more disturbing local news. I'd read a report in the *Guilford Courier* of an instance where a bi-racial family had been harassed in town by a white supremacist. The father of the family—understandably upset—submitted a 'Letter to the Editor' that described the feelings of anger, frustration, and helplessness that the incident had caused him.

Reading that account was disturbing. What the heck was happening in my town? Was this an isolated incident, divorced from the brewing CRT tiff, or might they somehow be related? It was impossible to say. But if this was a 'trend,' it was becoming dangerous. In response to that letter about White Supremacist harassment, a letter of advice appeared in the *Guilford Courier* from another familiar reader, a couple weeks later.

I would describe David Roberts as a bit of a right-wing 'gadfly.' I only know him through his published words, but I've been told he's not an unpleasant fellow. He has for years been sharing his worldview with readers of the *Guilford Courier*, through unsolicited thoughts, on nearly every conceivable topic (and seemingly as frequently as the paper allows). Depending upon one's ideological orientation, Roberts was either a clever right wing provocateur; an intransigent ideologue; or something in between. I never thought he intended malice. But his opinions routinely seem to drip with intolerance. I usually recognized his writing style within the first couple of sentences—and often skipped the rest of what I presumed would be predictable sophistry.

When counseling others, I'd noticed that Roberts could share the wisdom of the ages—such as advice that had been passed on to him from his mother when he was but a wee lad. He advised the bi-racial family to "tough up," and simply ignore those pesky white supremacists. There was also something in his letter about 'sticks and stones,' and 'broken bones,' and 'words' and such. I imagine his sagacious counsel provided that family with great comfort in their time of distress.

I'd also noticed Roberts wasn't always so measured. When he and his wife encountered "verbal abuse" from passing motorists—for holding 'Trump' signs on the roadside—he didn't "tough up" and ignore them. He wrote a 'Letter to the Editor' that likened the indignity they'd suffered to a "hate crime." In the wake of George Floyd's murder at the 'knee' of a Minneapolis police officer, he bemoaned 'Black Lives Matter' signs that were "popping up" in Guilford. He fretted about the effect those signs could have on the morale of Guilford's police officers. He warned that only a 'thin blue line' stood between Guilford and chaos, reminding all that "New Haven is only just down the street." Several readers angrily responded to his perceived racist trope (New Haven being a dog whistle code for 'where the people of color live').

Anyway, in summer of 2021, a right-wing band of BOE candidates had wrested control of the Republican Town Committee in Guilford, and was inciting an intellectual race riot. An esteemed Black judge, scholar and educator had been threatened, and warned to stay away from Guilford. A White Supremacist had reportedly harassed a local biracial family. During my 35 years in Guilford, any one of those developments would have set off serious alarm bells throughout the town. To have all three things happening, nearly simultaneously, seemed inconceivable. Suffice to say that I was definitely feeling unsettled, in advance of the upcoming election. And of course, I was still waiting for evidence of the big conspiracy to drop.

It was clear that the Guilford BOE had firmly aligned itself with the Connecticut State Department of Education's goal of '*improving the academic lives of Connecticut's increasingly diverse student body...*' To me that seemed like a reasonable and salutary objective. The argument could be made that fostering awareness of, and sensitivity to cultural and social differences, might be especially important in a town like Guilford, where actual opportunities to interact with and learn from a diverse student body are—let's be honest—somewhat limited.

Those in the CRT conspiracy camp continued to voice tired complaints about teachers reading controversial books. And some seemed to believe that the very mention of 'certain' facts in schools—such as the history of racism in America—would cause sensitive White children to feel guilty for the sins of others. Setting aside for a moment the incredible trauma that has been visited for centuries upon peoples of color; are we truly going to try to erase facts from our history books, because the events were so shameful that White kids might feel unease in hearing about them?

Perhaps we should abandon teaching *any* history, other than the glorious birth of the U.S.A.? Then we could freely analyze and discuss all of our founding documents, including the somewhat important U.S. Constitution. Of course, lest any White folks find it too sensitive a subject, we could choose to edit out the uncomfortable language, contained in the original document, that treated slaves as essentially 3/5 of a person. Here's a thought: Why not take it a step further, and just stop teaching all difficult subjects? Dumping calculus sure would have made my high school math career a lot easier.

As to the 'coincidence' that right-wing politicians throughout the country were claiming that within the span of just a few months, CRT—which in fact is an advanced academic framework taught in law schools—had suddenly become part of secondary school curricula everywhere? When I first heard about that, my thoughts immediately jumped to Will Rogers. Who could seriously believe that Democrats (i.e., Marxists) had the organizational wherewithal to pull off such a vast, nationwide conspiracy, almost overnight? Anyone who bought that claim obviously hadn't heeded the words of Will Rogers: "*I am not a member of any organized political party. I am a Democrat.*"

The CRT conspiracy felt like little more than a cynical (albeit perilous) contrivance.

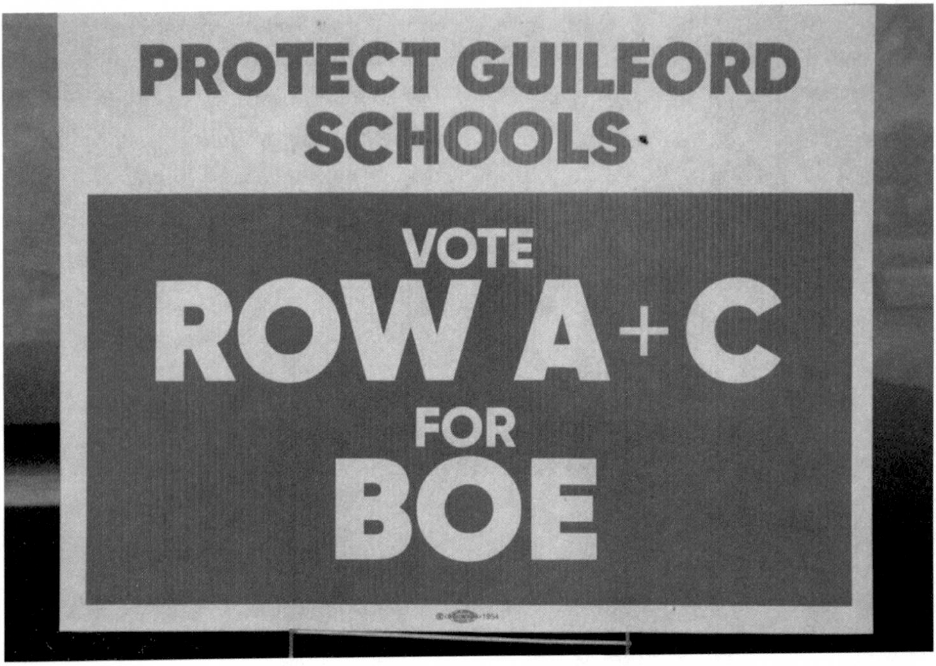
PROTECT GUILFORD
SCHOOLS
VOTE
ROW A+C
FOR
BOE

CHAPTER NINE

VOTE ROW A AND C FOR BOE

On August 26, 2021, when I saw my 'ad' hit the back page of the *Guilford Courier*, I immediately opened the paper, and rifled through it to see whether anyone else might have written a letter expressing similar disgust over the threat against Judge Robinson. The first letter that I spotted was from Mary Beeman. She was a former BOE member, and had been among the most prominent Republican voices in Guilford carping about CRT. She didn't mention the threat against Judge Robinson. Her letter was effusively in support of Nick Cusano—one of the endorsed Republican curriculum cops. She seemed quite impressed by him. Here's how her letter started:

> "Nick Cusano is a new friend that I wish I'd met years ago. One of the kindest, most intelligent men you would be proud to know, he has the determination of a pit bull when it comes to fighting Critical Race Theory in Guilford Public Schools…"
>
> —Mary Beeman (excerpt from *Guilford Courier* 'Letters to the Editor' dated 8/26/2021)

I thought: *Bless him…a 'pit bull' you say?' Gosh, when you put it like that, he does sound awfully 'kind.'* And the intelligence was manifest from his strategy. Fighting like a pit bull, against a foe that doesn't actually exist, would be a tough fight to lose. I just hoped that after the election—when silly season was over—the CRT conspiracy team would be freed up to channel their energies and talents to tackle more pressing issues, like keeping quantum physics out of kindergarten classes (I mean, those kids already have enough on their plates).

That same letter also offered up this startling claim:

"…I recently witnessed Nick's passion for our children and our town when he spoke extemporaneously for 10 minutes in front of a crowd glued to his every word about the movement in Guilford to expose the Marxist ideology that is no longer creeping, but careening into our children's classroom…"
—Mary Beeman (excerpt from *Guilford Courier* 'Letters to the Editor' dated 8/26/2021)

Marxist ideology? Not just creeping—but *careening*? Right into our kids' classrooms? I had to admit, that sounded pretty bad. Presumably at some point (hopefully soon), there would actually be some *evidence* produced to prove this conspiracy of careening Marxism. I mean, like *real* evidence—something more ascertainable than just a hearsay letter, fawning over Nick's stem-winder of a speech. It was late August. I figured some CRT conspiracy cop would be revealing the proof any day. I assumed it would at least be in time to influence the vote in the upcoming September primary.

That didn't happen.

There was no proof of Marxism careening through the hallways of our schools. A few more scary-sounding letters appeared in the paper over the next weeks, warning about the danger of CRT. In the face of such ominous warnings, about quisling teachers and administrators serving up Marxist ideology—many more letters appeared that were *in support of our educators*. That was a great relief to me, because I've always had the utmost respect for the teaching profession.

Teachers are overworked and underpaid. They are not in their chosen profession for money or power or personal attention. They teach for the noblest reason: they love kids, and helping them to learn and grow, as students and people. And every time I saw a letter cravenly parroting the CRT conspiracy accusations, and attacking educators and administrators, even though those letters were in the extreme minority, my stomach sank. That a handful of conspiracy theorists kept disparaging and defaming our teachers and educational administrators—the real heroes of our highly ranked school system—was exasperating.

I realized I'd have to be patient (hardly my strong suit). But surely some actual demonstrable proof would eventually be forthcoming. At that point, the residents of Guilford would be free to assess the conspiracy claims—kinda like jurors—and decide just how close we were to officially becoming a Marxist town. Meanwhile, CRT was becoming a hot-button issue, being trumpeted by far right politicians, throughout the country.

One of my daughters lives in Virginia. She told me that CRT had become a divisive issue in their Governor's race. As a cynical, purely political ploy, pitching a CRT conspiracy actually made a bit more sense in Virginia, than it did in Connecticut. Richmond, after all, had been the Capital of the Confederacy. Most of Virginia was a battlefield during the Civil War. With the recent ebb and flow of protests in that state over Confederate statues and symbols; and counter-protests over their proposed removal, I could see where race could be a particularly useful weapon for cynical Virginia politicians to wield in pursuit of power.

It was suspicious that the language about CRT, appearing in letters in our local paper, included buzzwords, and catch phrases, that seemed to have been 'cut-and-pasted' from the national right wing idiolect. I had to keep reminding myself that this was not Alabama…or Mississippi…or (name the bright red state). This was Connecticut…The Land of Steady Habits. This was Guilford, for Heaven's sake. A wild conspiracy theory couldn't gain traction here…*could it?*

The local GOP primary came and went in September, and I began to really worry when Guilford's Republican primary voters selected the five endorsed CRT curriculum cops—they would be the candidates vying for the five open seats on the BOE in our November election (Row 'B' on your ballot, for those keeping score at home). I kept thinking back to *Infinity Insurance Company*, and its infuriating overreach. Had the CRT curriculum cops in Guilford overreached? Was it possible that their platform—almost solely based upon their 'CRT-in-the-curriculum' claim—would be so toxic that <u>no</u> Republicans would be elected to the BOE in November? Even though Democrats and Independents significantly outnumbered Republicans in Guilford, such a result seemed unlikely, given the peculiar rules that govern our local school board elections.

The rules governing the Guilford Board of Education provide for nine positions, to be held by local citizens elected to serve unsalaried, staggered four-year terms. In what is commonly referred to as 'guaranteed *minority* representation' (there's a certain irony in that term), the rules also provide as follows: "*No party is allowed to hold more than a bare majority*" (of the nine seats). That meant no party could hold more than five seats. And in the 2021 election, five of the nine seats would be up for grabs.

This was all pretty dull, technical stuff. In past elections, most residents probably hadn't given those rules and numbers much thought (I know I hadn't). But 2021 had already proven itself to be a different kind of year. Given the minority representation rule, the five Republican candidates—who all entertained some pretty outlandish conspiracy theories—would be on the ballot in the upcoming election, running to fill the five open seats. Unfortunately (from my perspective), the ballot would NOT present to voters a simple, zero-sum choice, of voting for either the five Republican conspiracy theory team, on one row; or, an '*anyone-other-than-them*' option, on a second row. There might well be other candidates—but they would occupy other rows on the ballot. Splitting up one's choices would probably require a certain degree of voter awareness and deliberation.

Democrats already occupied three of the unexpired seats on the Board. That meant *only two Democrats* would be on the ballot. With five Republicans, running against two Democrats, for five open seats, it seemed quite likely that at least some if not most of the Republican endorsed candidates (the Row 'B' conspiracy cops) would win. Their frenzy could become a built-in, structural bomb, ticking within the BOE and the high-ranking school district of Guilford, Connecticut.

Out of curiosity, I took another peek at the popular '*Niche*' school rating service, which assigns grades to school systems in 6 separate categories. Guilford schools received an overall rating of 'A.' But not surprisingly, Guilford's grade in the '*Diversity*' category was a lowly 'C-'...which prompted me to think: *if the Row 'B' team really cared about improving our schools, they'd be spending their boundless energy helping to make kids of color feel more, not less welcome.*

Just after the five CRT conspiracy cops won the GOP primary, and took over Row 'B' on the ballot for the November election, something intriguing happened. A group of unaffiliated voters in town saw what was going on—and then stepped up and created another option for Guilford voters. The November ballot would instruct voters that they could vote for up to five candidates, for the five open BOE positions. There would be two Democrats running for re-election (they were current Board members whose terms had expired), and they would be on Row 'A' of the ballot. The five Republican CRT conspiracy candidates would occupy Row 'B.' Unaffiliated voters in town coalesced around three candidates, and they would appear on Row 'C' of the ballot, listed as '*Independents*.'

That development seemed to at least potentially give disillusioned voters a tolerable place to land. If they were turned off by the conspiracy platform pushed by the Republican-endorsed slate on Row 'B', they could vote for the three Independents on Row 'C.' Soon after that, another interesting, and frankly heart-warming development occurred. A town-wide movement emerged: residents were openly being encouraged to vote for Row 'A' and Row 'C' together. Before long, that idea seemed to be (dare I say it?) '*careening*' through town. If the candidates on Row 'A' and Row 'C' together, could garner more combined votes than the Row 'B' crew, Guilford voters could prevent any of the conspiracy candidates from infecting our school board.

As encouraging as that movement was, it didn't change the fact that this was still an off-year election, and turnout could be very low, based on recent history. With no other issues on the ballot, was it wishful thinking to expect a very high turnout in the November 2021 election, in Guilford, Connecticut? More than that, it would be a heavy lift to expect a large percentage of the voters who did turn out to do the math, and then apportion their votes in such a way as to defeat all five Row 'B' fabulists. That would be tough. But not impossible. Especially if people were tuned in, and paying attention to the distasteful events that had been occurring in town over the past several months. The stakes felt high for the seemingly mundane task of electing a new school board.

Before long, I began to notice a few lawn signs popping up around town that urged residents to '*VOTE ROW A & C for BOE*.' Soon, I noticed lots of those signs, on lots of lawns—and even in front of some local shops and businesses. Most encouraging of all to me were the signs that were posted on the properties of neighbors I knew to be long-time 'traditional' Republicans. That gave me hope—as well as a not-small degree of pride in my town.

Were there some zealous culture warriors? Of course. But there were many more moderate, open minds—which reminded me anew, that my wife Cathy and I originally moved to Guilford because of its charm, beauty and history; and we had stayed for decades, because of its people. Still though, given the structural advantage that the minority representation rule gave to the CRT conspiracy cops—with only two Democrats running against five Republicans—it would take a remarkable degree of voter engagement and turnout, in an 'off-year' election, to defeat the entire conspiracy team.

CHAPTER TEN

WAIT...WHAT?

As the '*Row A & C*' movement picked up steam, I waited patiently (wink) for bombshell evidence of '*careening*' Marxism. It didn't show up in September, or even early October. As the election neared, I wondered whether a late-October surprise might be in the works, with evidence to be 'dumped' just before the election. But that didn't happen.

Not surprisingly, there were some angry complaints from, and on behalf of, the Republican Row 'B' candidates, alleging a fraudulent radical left-wing conspiracy (yesiree...*another* conspiracy). This one apparently involved the three Independent candidates on Row 'C,' and the two Democrats on Row 'A'. Soon, a few cheeky signs popped up, proclaiming: '*A+C = Fraud*.' It seemed as though the whole town was abuzz, and just trying to keep track of the cascading conspiracy claims. But then, something else happened that pretty much sucked the air out of all those quaint conspiracy debates for a while.

What happened in October was the reporting of 18 words that had been attributed to the Row 'B' conspiracy team's campaign manager (Mary Beeman). They weren't 18 words that had been whispered privately, or offered in hushed tones at some Secret Society meeting. They weren't words that had been 'misattributed,' or misquoted by some scheming reporter with an obviously Marxist agenda. They were, in fact, the Row 'B' campaign manager's *actual words*.

During a presumably unguarded moment, she had offered them up while participating in an educational forum, sponsored by the University of Connecticut—our state's flagship institution. They were recorded, for all to see and contemplate. Here's what she had to say, while explaining the convoluted CRT conspiracy theory, and the fear of 'equity in education' in Guilford:

"Helping kids of color to feel they belong has a negative effect on white, Christian, or conservative kids."

Wait…__*WHAT?*__

Everyone who read those words got a quick education about the conspiracy crew's (previously) secret concerns. That language didn't sound like traditional 'conservatism.' It sounded closer to some version of White Christian Nationalism that *Fox News* pitchman Tucker Carlson might spew. Despite the almost religious fervor that the CRT conspiracy theorists seemed to share, to my ear those 18 words had a decidedly 'un-Christian' ring to them. Our church (First Congregational) proudly proclaims: "*No matter who you are, you are welcome here.*" I certainly hope that doesn't mean our ancient church has radical Marxist underpinnings?

I'm not a theological scholar, and I don't quote Scripture. I hope those facts alone don't disqualify me from offering an observation (after all, according to Shakespeare, *even the devil can cite Scripture for his purpose*). I seem to recall reading *somewhere* that the Prince of Peace was tolerant, welcoming and accepting. I thought: *Seriously? Is being welcoming and tolerant a zero-sum game to these new-age White Christian conservatives? Do they only have enough tolerance in their hearts to welcome the 9 out of every 10 kids in Guilford who are White? Rough break for you 1 out of 10 kids who are 'of color.' Y'all are flat out of luck if your parents vote for us.*

As a starting point that must be acknowledged as a fundamental truth to many: White Christian conservatives have never done anything to hurt anyone. Well…except for that whole slavery business. That was pretty mean—as has been the treatment of indigenous people since our earliest days. Oh, and Jim Crow segregation, which wasn't too nice either. And admittedly that '*Ku Klux Klan*' outfit wasn't the best foot forward for White Christian conservatives.

That's all ancient history of course. But the important point now is that it's always been the radical 'liberal' rascals who have stirred the pot, and upset the comfy social order for White people. That's why White Christian conservatives need protection *now*, as much as ever. Let's not forget, it was those pesky 19th century abolitionists who pushed to free the slaves. If it hadn't been for them, we would never have had a Civil War. The White Christian conservatives, that mostly ran the slaveholding southern states, were practically forced to secede, in the face of a tyrannical federal government, threatening to infringe upon their God-given freedom to hold Black people in bondage.

If that wasn't enough, the radical lefties then advocated for suffrage for '*certain*' people of color…and then for '*certain*' women…and then even for '*women of color,*' of all things! The 13th and 14th and 15th and 19th Amendments; Voting Rights Act; Civil Rights Act. All these protections, for *all people*! Gracious, when will it end? White

Christian conservatives won't have a chance, unless we take a firm stance now…and refuse to allow kids of color…to feel they belong…in the nice, mostly White Town of Guilford.

Okay, never mind all that. The point is…Oh heck—I have absolutely no idea what the Row 'B' campaign manager's point was? None of those words made any sense to me. Quite frankly, even Lee Atwater in his heyday—say around the time he was devising Nixon's 'southern strategy,' which turned Dixiecrats into Republican voters—probably would have counseled a bit more circumspection (although Atwater's notion of employing 'dog-whistles,' to appeal to the basest of human instincts, seems almost quaint by today's standards—when foghorns seem to be the instrument of choice). Should politicians today get away with saying the really shocking stuff out loud? Several had been doing so for years on a national stage, and in certain parts of the country. The people of Guilford would soon have a say as to how much intolerance a moderate New England town would tolerate.

CHAPTER ELEVEN

GUILFORD DOESN'T DO CRAZY

A lthough I don't know her personally, I have heard—and fully believe—that there is abundant kindness and intelligence in Mary Beeman. And yet, I must admit, I find bewildering many of her published words. As to those particular 18 words, there was an awful lot to unpack there. I tried to imagine some conceivable argument that could be mustered in support of her theory, which I might describe as the 'Critical Of Nice Children Of Color Theory' ('*CONCOCT*') for short. According to the *CONCOCT-ion*, when kids of color are made to feel welcome, it somehow has a "*negative effect*" on white, Christian or conservative kids. I decided to break that theory down, starting with the first part, as it relates to 'white kids.'

As anyone who knows nothing about the history of race since the earliest days of the American Colonies will tell you, White people have had it rough here in America from day one; while people of color have had things pretty easy. I mean sure, over 4 centuries ago, Black people were brought to these shores in chains. True, over the following centuries, millions of Black people were held in bondage, and had families broken apart. Yes, they were forced to work for no pay…but that was just an early example of fiscal conservatism at work. Seriously, why would any prudent business-owner suffer recurring labor costs, when he could simply 'invest' in human beings, shackle them, and force them to work for nothing?

None of that ancient history should even matter now. Didn't everything pretty much change on a dime after the Emancipation Proclamation, the end of the Civil War, and then the passage of the 13th Amendment? (Discounting, of course, the next quick century, with 'Jim Crow' segregation, and rampant beatings and lynchings and such). But after *that*, the Civil Rights Act and the Voting Rights Act were passed in the 1960's.

So there you have it!

It is no longer a crime in any state to teach Black people to read or write. Since 1967 (thanks to the Earl Warren Supreme Court) marriage between the races is no longer illegal anywhere in America. Heck, even Alabama deleted its (unenforceable) miscegenation law from the books in 2000, which is a sure sign of progress. So now, thankfully everything's just fine…nothin' to see here…let's move along. And let's definitely not talk about race… ever again…*ever*! Cuz ya know—talking about race is surely a Marxist tell.

Okay, maybe *CONCOCT-ion* wasn't totally convincing as to 'white kids.' But it had a point, in terms of local history, since Guilford is now 'only' around 90% White. That's quite a drop-off in 'Whiteness' since 1639, when Guilford was presumably almost 100% White (save for possibly a few early slaves—and those pesky Natives who were politely negotiated off of their native land). So here we are, left to grapple with the classic slippery slope that the far right disdains: If we continue on the dangerous path of allowing kids of color to feel they belong, there's just no telling what Guilford might look like in another 4 centuries or so.

Right…never mind that incomprehensible first part of the *CONCOCT-ion*. Moving on to the second part of the CRT conspiracy theory, as it relates to '*Christian kids*'…*Yes! Of course!* That must somehow make sense…cuz it's gotta be pretty darn intimidating for any Christian kid to grow up and go to school in Guilford. I mean sure, the Guilford Town Green is ringed with Christian churches of various denominations (not to mention numerous affiliated parish outbuildings). And it seems that not a single Mosque or Temple exists within Guilford's borders. Still, a pretty strong argument can be made that it's really tough out there to be a Christian kid…in a predominantly Christian town like Guilford…especially if kids of color are made to feel like they belong. Said no one. Ever. Other than the CRT conspiracy squad's campaign manager.

All right…so also never mind that second, also befuddling part. All of the sense must lie hidden, deep within *CONCOCT-ion's* third category, which deals with 'conservative kids.' I confess, I have no idea what it means to be a 'conservative kid?' Maybe it's a kid whose parents have less than 'traditional' interpretations of Christianity? Frankly I'm not even sure what it means these days to be a 'conservative?' Years ago, I thought I had a handle on it. They were fine with: a tip-top school system (which we have); and fire and police departments fully equipped, and staffed by well-trained, consummate professionals (which we have); and streets, sidewalks and a town green that were tidy and clean (which we have). They just really hated those darn taxes (which we have). But that only went to part of conservative orthodoxy. And I truly did understand the 'fiscal' side of conservatism.

I've always agreed with fiscal conservatives as to a general proposition: an appropriate degree of fiscal restraint is essential. I haven't always agreed with them as to what's 'appropriate,' and have often come down on the other side of the spending equation. For instance, several years ago, Guilford taxpayers were endlessly debating the merits of building a new high school—as opposed to repairing the multiple roof leaks that for years had plagued the moldy old structure. I'm pretty sure the fiscal conservatives were the ones who wanted to basically patch up, or at most replace, the old roof.

Spending money to patch up an antiquated, decrepit and unhealthy school building didn't seem wise to me. But the 'when' and 'why' of it all was a legitimate and traditional subject for healthy debate. An historical footnote: In my opinion the state-of-the-art high school that was eventually approved, and then finally built, is spectacular. Although all three of my kids had graduated long before it opened, I still viewed it as a wonderful investment in future generations of Guilford's kids.

I hesitate to here make an observation about the 'national' GOP brand, for fear that I might begin to come across as preachy, and judgmental.

Right…too late for that. (I am nothing, if not self-aware).

So…as to the national Republican Party's brand of 'neo-conservatism,' with its near-talismanic focus on 'social issues' and 'culture wars?' I'm definitely not on board that train—which seems to have left the station years ago, and without anyone firmly at the controls. Granted, the national GOP has long been comprised of an awkward mélange of disparate, single-issue bedfellows. These days, it's easy to see in which direction their train is heading (here's a hint: it's to the *RIGHT*). But now, it's difficult to divine who's actually running that train?

Hopefully, it's not the '*engineers*'…of the January 6th insurrection; or the Q-Anon cabal; or the White Supremacist/White Nationalist sect. Maybe it will end up being those political nihilists who've used the democratic electoral system to get elected to Congress—with the avowed goal of blowing up that very system? It could even be the religious right, whose 'devout' bargain with the devil has already paid off handsomely in a few lifetime Supreme Court Seats (nothing says 'small-government conservatism' more than supporting: a legislative branch of the government—comprised mostly of White men—that determines, and then tells women, what they may do with their bodies; an executive branch, that enforces those instructions; and judges who obligingly say '*yup…looks good to us*').

Fortunately…*Guilford doesn't do crazy*! Guilford has thrived, throughout many challenging periods in history, because it has always had a robust population of 'traditional' Republicans. Those intrepid souls have steadfastly resisted, and when necessary, stood up to the worst instincts exhibited on the national scene.

CHAPTER TWELVE

KITTENS ARE CUTE...
RAINBOWS ARE PRETTY...

When I began trying to piece together the baffling Guilford CRT conspiracy puzzle in the fall of 2021, things didn't add up. The evidence seemed contrary to the Row 'B' conspiracy theorists' contention. By all credible accounts, CRT was not, and had never been, part of the Guilford school curriculum. And when I read reporting in the fall of 2021, that a good percentage of the Row 'B' squad's campaign money had come from out-of-town sources (reportedly *over 40%*—an historically unheard-of amount), my skepticism only grew.

I was also bothered by the suspicious 'coincidence' that the language used by the local CRT conspiracy theorists had seemingly been plucked out of a national playbook. Were they following some sort of right-wing guide on how to incite an intellectual race riot? Some right-wing media outlets, including *Fox* and *Breitbart*, even singled out little Guilford, Connecticut, as a town where CRT was the main issue being contested in the 2021 election.

In other words, the national disease appeared to have infected Guilford. Whether it would metastasize, as it had in other parts of the country, became anyone's guess. But it was an unsettling time for people like me, who had thought Guilford was impervious to the most narrow-minded of conservative social '*values*.' And unfortunately, the best hope to defeat the race-baiting power play that was being urged upon us would require voter engagement, and then turnout, of historic proportions.

After the predictable and widespread condemnation that followed the reporting of Row 'B' campaign manager's '18 words,' she backpedalled into an awkward '*sort-of* apology, which itself was more befuddling than edifying. She attempted to clarify things, by releasing a statement to explain that the 18 words she'd offered to the world were basically the *opposite* of how she really felt about all of God's children. She didn't exactly elucidate why she'd uttered words that were the opposite of what she meant. In an October 14, 2021 article in the *Guilford Courier* that reported on her 'statement,' she described her earlier words as "*clumsy*." She reportedly claimed that her words had been '*taken out of context.*' The furrows on the brows of most residents were probably symptomatic of the struggle to divine any conceivable context in which those 18 words would not seem intolerant and offensive.

I naively expected that when the dust settled, the CRT conspiracy theorists would give their campaign manager the boot, for having said 'out loud' the part that they presumably would have preferred to keep quiet. But despite widespread outrage, that didn't happen either. Although the five candidates themselves remained unnervingly quiet amid the furor, their campaign manager reported that she enjoyed their full support. And the more I thought about those 18 words, the more something kept tickling at my memory. I dug through my 'archives,' and found the August 26, 2021 edition of the *Guilford Courier*—the one that contained my back-page 'ad.' I re-read Mary Beeman's letter. It had included this paragraph about her 'kind' new friend Nick 'the-pit-bull' Cusano:

> "...*He is the first to tell you that the administration's smoke screen will be exposed very soon when he is elected to the Board of Education. His children, both at Guilford High School this year, and a number of their friends have experienced firsthand how the Equity and Social Justice Initiative is code for 'silence the conservative voices in the room...'*"
> —Mary Beeman (8/26/2021 excerpt from *Guilford Courier* 'Letters to the Editor')

That letter, in alleging a secret 'code' about silencing the 'conservative voices in the room,' was interesting for what it did *not* say. It conspicuously didn't say a single thing about silencing 'White voices.' Nor did it mention silencing 'Christian voices.' It only talked about 'conservative voices.' And that actually made a bit more sense to me, whereas the infamous words about 'white kids' and 'Christian kids,' in a predominantly White Christian town, had made literally no sense whatsoever.

That was when it occurred to me that the right-wing CRT conspiracy theory being pitched in Guilford—using the national right-wing playbook, its language, and perhaps its money—might be a charade. The CRT conspiracy claims didn't seem to have much of anything to do with our actual school 'curriculum.' I'd been waiting for evidence...anxious to weigh the facts. But with the Row 'B' crowd, there wasn't really a factual predicate. They seized upon a national right-wing strategy, and stirred up the CRT 'controversy.' Then they promised to make it all go away. CRT wasn't part of the Guilford school curriculum, according to people in positions to know.

All that stuff raised the question-of-the-hour (or year): Why confuse and mischaracterize things, to create a controversy that didn't actually exist? Was the real goal to force more 'conservative' voices onto the school board? If so, then why not just own it? Why the whole race-baiting sideshow? It felt to me as though this was the blatant use of race, as a means to an end, by people who were self-described 'social conservatives.' Was race being employed as a wedge, to garner power? And if so? Why race?

Dr. Martin Luther King famously said: "A riot is the language of the unheard." Being White, or being Christian…in Guilford…obviously put them in the majority. On the other hand, being new-age 'social conservatives' placed these folks in the minority. Did these social conservatives feel unheard?

Trying to pitch their hard-right, conservative social beliefs probably wasn't in itself an effective route to power in a moderate and welcoming town like Guilford. Was the goal to shake-up residents, and try to get them worried enough, that they might ignore facts, and accept ominous conspiracy theories instead? Had they manufactured a conspiracy that *they* thought sounded frightening enough that it would move people to action? It sure felt like a cynical ploy. Could such a thing succeed in Guilford?

Kittens are cute, and rainbows are pretty. But psychologists know that primordial *FEAR* is the greatest motivator of human behavior. That's a lesson that the far right has learned well. Stoking fear to garner power has been a tactic that it's mastered, over many years. The cynical calculation in Guilford may have been—as it seems to have been throughout much of the country—that there's nothing more frightening to White people than the thought of people of color feeling welcome and engaged.

Did they think that embellishments, conflations and confusion might convince people of something that they (the conspiracy theorists) thought sounded frightening—something about race and our kids? Did they assume that the residents of Guilford—a predominantly White town—would just accept their claims, and vote for them, out of some sort of blind racial fear? If so, that sure didn't seem like a customary appeal to traditional conservatives. Whatever the motivation for peddling a racially charged conspiracy theory about the school curriculum in Guilford…to me it felt like a dangerous play.

(We're all in this together, so....)

It's a Dunk Rock Road (DRR) Block Party

Saturday October 2, 2021

CHAPTER THIRTEEN

THROUGH THE 'MARXIST LENS' LOOKING-GLASS

Despite the outcome of the primary that put the CRT conspiracy cops on the ballot, I still had confidence in the people of Guilford. I told myself: one coward anonymously told Judge Robinson she wouldn't be welcome; a small fringe objected to equity and social justice in our schools. But most residents of Guilford are warm and welcoming. Then the 2021 edition of our local block party bolstered my confidence even more.

Due to the pandemic, it had been a couple years since our street had held its fall block party. In early October 2021 (about a month before the election), that tradition resumed. It was the most fun I'd had in a while. It was a chance to catch up with old neighbors, and meet new ones. At the end of the evening, after the merriment was over and Cathy and I had retired to our home, we marveled at the diversity of our little street.

We live on a small road that begins at the south side of the Boston Post Road, within sight of the iconic *Bishop's Orchards Farm Market*. Founded in 1871, *Bishop's* is routinely voted one of Connecticut's top farm markets. Our road is about ½ mile long, ending just past the entrance to the 'West Woods' hiking trails and *Bishop's Orchards* raspberry fields (the 'pick-your-own' raspberry season was still in full swing when our block party took place).

We have interesting and eclectic neighbors. Although we'd lived in the same house for nearly 35 years, we weren't the longest tenured residents on our road. Since the pandemic began, several new families had moved in, and the 2021 Block Party was a chance to meet some of them. There were some 'old timers' like us but also several new and young families. Kids were racing around and playing together, while adults were meeting new neighbors for the first time. I came away from the evening with my faith in Guilford fully restored. The intolerant few, whose letters I'd read over the previous months, seemed anomalous. They were free to hold and share their opinions. But I was confident that those opinions weren't representative of the collective ethos of Guilford, Connecticut.

The morning after our block party, two of our newest neighbors, whom we'd met for the first time the night before (who originally hailed from Spain and Italy and had lived throughout Europe), shared through our neighborhood e-mail chain that they'd never felt more welcomed. I was buoyed reading those words, and marveled at how simple a gesture it is to make others feel welcome; and how much positive energy those simple gestures can generate. Unfortunately, a few days later, another of David Roberts' letters to the *Guilford Courier* popped my happy-place balloon. Soon enough, I was composing my own opinion letter in response (after 34 years in town, that was a first for me), while wondering whether I was becoming a gadfly?

Here's my letter, as published in the October 21, 2021 *Guilford Courier:*

Even in Guilford

Dave Roberts is 'confused' again, which should surprise nobody [Oct. 7 letter "Confess to be Confused"]. His style is familiar, albeit formulaic (almost Seussian). He picks a position with which he disagrees, constructs a tortured deduction, then wonders what he's missing. Here's how it works: State "Some Board of Education candidates recently fabricated a political/racial issue. Now they promise they'll stop Critical Race Theory (CRT) and politics in Our Schools. By not supporting them, I'm a Marxist, right?" Fun game. Anyone can play.

The CRT contretemps wasn't on Roberts's radar on October 7. He was too confused by "virtue-signaling lawn signs," but desires explication. I'll try: Whether inspirational, aspirational, welcoming, threatening, lawn-signs are mere symbols. They assume a basic degree of common sense. No, a "Peace" sign doesn't end all conflict. No, equity doesn't mean everyone gets A's. Yes, Caucasians can welcome diverse neighbors, even in Guilford.

I mostly ignore the silliness, but the October 7 display of cynicism was breathtaking. Roberts proclaimed that if we welcome neighbors with signs containing different languages/colors, we're hypocrites: "This," he wrote, "from people who for some reason have chosen to live in a town as non-diverse as Guilford." Wow, busted. We chose Guilford to avoid those others. We thought a virtue-signaling sign might fool people. Roberts saw through our charade.

As Roberts wrote his latest letter, we attended our neighborhood 'block-party,' sharing food, drink and fellowship with neighbors of diverse backgrounds, skin-tones, and orientations. We have neighbors of Italian, Spanish, Ecuadorian, Columbian, Jamaican, Portuguese, Asian descent—and more. The symphony of laughter and accents was comforting. On October 3, two new neighbors, in a beautiful email, offered that they'd lived in 10 places (6 countries) and had never felt more welcomed. Imagine that? In Guilford no less!

(Greg Kinsella—Guilford, CT)

We were weeks from Election Day, and every time I thought the crazy talk might be waning, I'd see another letter (like Mr. Roberts' latest intellectual razing of lawn signs) that would make me wonder all over again what was happening in my town? For the record, Cathy was quite proud of the sign that she'd purchased, which contains inter-locking hands of different skin tones and proclaims: '*All Are Welcome Here.*' That sign had survived countless Nor'easters, blizzards and tropical storms (the worst of which knocked out power for 4 days).

With a few keystrokes, Roberts had dismissed our sign, and others like it, as sheer hypocrisy. He was essentially saying: who could believe that any Guilford resident would actually '*welcome*' anyone who looks a bit different, or speaks a bit differently? Recall it was Roberts who'd once likened having been heckled over his 'Trump' sign to a 'hate crime.' But he seemed to have no qualms about metaphorically heckling every *virtue-signaling sign*-owner in town. I don't know the guy or his motivations. Maybe he chooses to live in Guilford because of its lack of diversity? Perhaps it never occurred to him that anyone might do so in spite of it?

That latest display of cynicism had been published right around the time that Row 'B' campaign manager had instigated shocked reactions throughout town for her infa-mous 18 words, which implied that kids of color shouldn't be made to feel welcome. Those socially conservative challenges—to the very act of welcoming someone—reminded me of the threat that had been made against Judge Robinson: that anonymous email, in which she'd been warned that she was '*not welcome in Guilford,*' and that she would meet '*great resistance*' if she dared return. That very premise, and some of the language, had been similar to the words of David Roberts and Mary Beeman—so much so that I wondered whether they all belonged to the same Secret Society?

I couldn't wait for the election. At the same time, I feared what might be unleashed if the voters of Guilford didn't turn out en masse to reject the dangerous CRT canard. One thing that did occur to me was the self-contained irony within the First Amendment, which allows freedom of speech—and therefore allows people the freedom to share all manner of narrow-minded ideas. Words can be dangerous. They can be hurtful. They can signal—if not outright encourage—the acceptance of intolerance. We ignore intolerant words at our peril. Better to confront them head on, with our own words. As much as I'd prefer that intolerant theories not drive up my blood pressure, the 1st Amendment doesn't allow us to silence those opinions. Ironically, that fact can provide a secondary benefit.

Every once in a while, people will open their mouths (or laptops, or phones) and tell everyone what they're thinking. Some coward had done so anonymously against Judge Robinson. Mr. Roberts does it all the time. The Row 'B' campaign manager had done so rather infamously. The fact that certain 'opinions' had actually been stated/written/printed publicly, for all to consider…well maybe that was exactly what was needed to wake us all up, like a cold slap in the face (as had happened to me in August), and force us to take notice…and then hopefully take action? And speaking of waking up…

Around that same time, something else occurred to me. I realized that I might have become something known in certain circles as "*woke.*" I wasn't fully up-to-speed as to the far-right patois, but I was pretty sure being 'woke' had become one of their favorite *insults du jour*? I knew the term had benign historical roots, but I figured its current iteration was not intended to be complimentary. Of late, it definitely seemed to have a pejorative connotation (especially since it was coming from the mouths of people who were self-styled '*anti-woke*' patriots).

Being 'woke' seemed to have something to do with being attentive to important societal issues—maybe even to the degree of sensing and expressing repugnance over things that were…well…morally repugnant. I figured Abe Lincoln would probably have qualified as 'woke' by the time he was serving as our 16th president. By then, his lifelong opposition to slavery had crystallized into a stubborn realization: slavery was not just an uncomfortable truth in America; it was an evil institution that was morally repugnant to the very conceits of the Declaration of Independence and basic humanity—and therefore no longer tolerable in America, morally or legally.

Being '*anti-woke*' didn't strike me as a very informative description of what the opponents of '*wokeness*' actually stood for? Maybe '*hibernatin*'—or some such thing—might be a more apt portrayal? I decided it was better to be morally *woke* than morally *hibernatin*,' so I was okay with it. Plus, if it would have been good enough for Honest Abe, it was certainly fine with me.

Anyway, as Election Day neared in Guilford, I observed an interesting development. A couple letters in the *Courier* seemed to *redefine* 'curriculum' in the context of the CRT conspiracy theory. I saw (grudging) concessions that perhaps CRT '*per se*' wasn't being taught, followed by the theory that our educators had ostensibly been brainwashed. They had read controversial books. That—according to the conspiracy theorists—meant those teachers must now unknowingly be teaching any controversial ideologies contained therein.

That prompted an unsettling recollection. I had once read passages from *Mein Kampf* for a college course on the rise of Hitler. I really hope reading those hideous words hadn't turned me into an unwitting anti-Semite or Nazi? Just to be safe in Guilford, perhaps we should require a compendium of every book that every one of our teachers has ever read? Then we could let the Row 'B' conspiracy crew determine what dangerous notions might be floating around inside all those gullible heads? Apparently, the argument was that our teachers had been '*re-educated*' (i.e. brainwashed), so that they now all saw the world through the '*lens*' of Marxism. Therefore, Marxist principles were leaching into lesson plans, through the subconscious (or worse) leanings of those gullible, indoctrinated teachers.

Frankly, it all seemed a bit far-fetched to me. But at least it was a tacit admission that there had been no evidence produced in support of the actual CRT-in-the-curriculum theory (which was basically the sole platform upon which the Row 'B' candidates for the Board of Education were running). In fact, soon after those '*Marxist lens*' letters had appeared in the *Guilford Courier,* we received in the mail a fancy, glossy flier. It had been mailed by some committee of which Nick Cusano (a/k/a 'Pit bull') was treasurer. In bright, bold, and urgent letters and symbols, that mailer referred to the "*Row C extremists!*" It implored residents to "*Vote ANYONE BUT ROW C.*" I wondered whether it had been an oversight that there was no mention of the two Democrats on Row A? Had they already lost their 'extremist' standing? Anyway, the fancy flier did explain this interesting CRT conspiracy nugget: "*CRT is not a class that is taught to the students but rather a lens or philosophy that is woven through a student's entire educational experience.*" It also described a dark "*process of re-education of the faculty*" through the books they had read.

Perhaps those fancy fliers were funded by the Row 'B' team's infusion of out-of-town money? I figured they must have been pretty flush with cash. If they had bothered to read my back-page ad about Judge Angela C. Robinson; or even my response to Dave Roberts' confusion over 'virtue-signaling' lawn signs; Nick's committee would have probably saved that postage. I suppose our receipt of that mailer may have at least signified one thing: Apparently I had yet to achieve official 'gadfly' status.

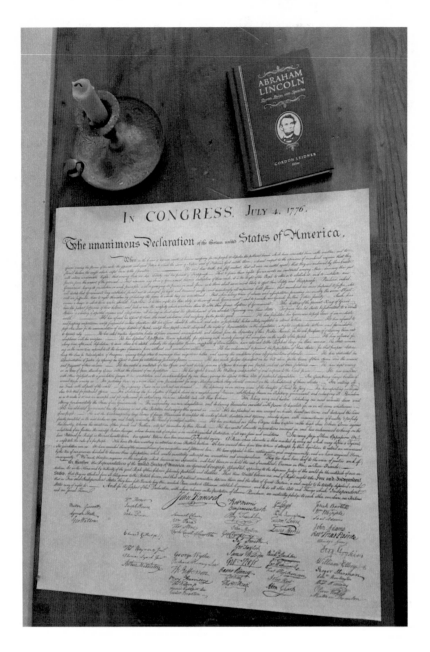

Now is Our Chance To STOP Indoctrination in Critical Race Theory

and other divisive initiatives. <u>We must teach our students how to think, not what to think.</u>

The extremists on Row C refuse to defend our kids against those who say our kids are racist. They continue to defend the office of Family Equity Liaison. Our kids are not racist, and we won't stand by and let them be treated as such.

Row C extremists have no right to call our kids and families racist, <u>enough is enough</u>.

Vote
ANYONE BUT ROW C
For Guilford Board of Education

Now Showing in a Public School Near You!

CRITICAL RACE THEORY

The assertion that CRT (Critical Race Theory) is not being taught in Guilford Public Schools is nonsense.

What ROW C extremists are not telling you is that CRT is not a class that is taught to the students but rather a lens, a philosophy that is woven through a student's entire educational experience.

Guilford Public Schools has started this process of re-education of the faculty in the philosophies of "Waking up White". That book was purchased with taxpayers funds and teachers across the district were told to read it.

I have read both "White Fragility" and "Waking Up White" with our leadership team... I provided a copy of "How To Be An Anti-Racist" to all teachers in our District...

email from Guilford Superintendent, 8/27/2020

Say no to indoctrination. Say no to hate.
Say no to Critical Race Theory.

SAY NO TO ROW C

CHAPTER FOURTEEN

THAT DOG WON'T HUNT IN GUILFORD

november 2, 2021—Election Day—dawned bright and crisp. A friend had asked me to volunteer a few hours of my time at a polling place, as a 'poll stander' (basically just welcoming people to the polls), and I'd signed up for an afternoon shift at a polling place in the northern part of town. In the morning, Cathy and I walked down the street to our polling place, which was *A. W. Cox School*. It was the same elementary school that all 3 of our kids had attended. Fortunately they'd all made it through Guilford's public school system before the Marxist take-over (and with that good Guilford public school education under their belts, they all went on to pursue advanced graduate degrees).

As we walked toward the entrance to the school, we were startled by a man who suddenly appeared between some bushes at the edge of the parking lot. He ominously beseeched us to "Vote for Row 'B,'" which elicited puzzled stares from us. Then he said: "anyone but the Row 'C' radicals." He offered us a flier, which we declined (I'm pretty sure it was the fancy flier we'd gotten in the mail). Then I gave him the bad news: we were "all-in with the radicals." With that, he silently retreated.

"Do you s'pose," I later said to Cathy, "that that Row 'B' disciple thought there were people who would actually go to the trouble of showing up at the polls…with no idea for whom they planned to vote? And that they would then make their decisions based on the advice offered by some scary dude popping out from between the bushes?" It seemed like an awfully bizarre campaign strategy. We agreed that it had been the weirdest Election Day moment we'd ever experienced during our many years in Guilford. That, of course, made perfect sense in the year 2021.

The couple of hours that I spent as a 'poll stander' on Election Day gave me a bit of optimism. For one thing, voter activity at the school where I was volunteering seemed quite brisk. Beyond that, reports from other polling places all over town were that the voter turnout was unusually high, compared to 'normal' off-year elections. Then again, this was anything but a *normal* election. It was only 10 months after the January 6th insurrection and attempted coup in Washington, D.C. It was also in theory a referendum on how the residents of Guilford viewed the cynical, racially charged CRT conspiracy theory that had become the local Republican plank for the past several months.

I got some text messages after the polls had closed that suggested a favorable outcome (from my perspective). The early 'unofficial' word was that all five Row 'B' conspiracy candidates appeared to have lost by sizable margins. After the year that had just passed, I was heartened. All the same, in this weird year I was still too anxious to 'breathe easy' until I could see something 'official.' When I opened the *New Haven Register* the following day, and found the article about the results of the Guilford Board of Education contest, I felt major relief, and unbridled pride in my little Town.

Of course, the article mentioned the embarrassing and contentious CRT debate that had been fomented by the Row 'B' candidates. Guilford appeared to have been the most conspicuous victim in Connecticut of that right-wing CRT conspiracy maneuver. Thankfully the voters of Guilford had turned out in droves, to oppose the unproven accusations of those that had taken over control of the Guilford Republican Town Committee. The Row 'B' candidates had been clobbered by 2 to 1 margins across the board—a defeat of historic proportions in Guilford.

In the *previous* off-year election (2019), where there had been no such *exciting* issues on the ballot (*ahem*), Guilford voter turnout had only been around 20%. What about in 2021—the crazy year of the intellectual race riot in Guilford—where CRT conspiracy accusations were front-and-center? When the town-by-town voter turnout tallies were reported, Guilford was *over 60%*. That was far-and-away the *highest in the state* (and more than double the state-wide average).

As word of the election results spread, friends near and far reached out to us to express their relief, and also their praise for the sensible and tolerant Guilford electorate. Although some of the voices that had been raised in support of the Row 'B' crowd had been strident, they had also been relatively few. And I was quite sure, based upon nothing but my personal 'sense' of the people of Guilford, that a large percentage of those who actually voted for the Row 'B' candidates had done so simply because they always voted Republican.

Because of an anonymous threat against Judge Angela C. Robinson, my previous 'tune out' strategy was not an option for me in 2021. But it would have been understandable for registered Republican voters in Guilford to simply ignore the noise. They may not have believed the conspiracy theory. They may have simply cast their usual votes, for their party's endorsed slate.

The fact that so many Guilford voters across the political spectrum had bothered to show up at the polls—and then allocated their votes in such a way as to keep the Row 'B' conspiracy theorists away from our school board—was heartwarming to me to say the least. We may not be a very diverse town. But most of our residents are hospitable. The strategy of conflating and embellishing—about divisive racial issues no less—and the apparent attempt to normalize intolerance for political gain? If those were intentional strategies, thankfully they were soundly defeated at the polls by the voters of Guilford. For that I feel eternally grateful.

The fact of the matter is that a right-wing 'culture war' strategy—which was ultimately successful in the Virginia Governor's race—crashed and burned in Guilford. That result should have been viewed as a catastrophic outcome for the local Republican Party. After all, such a result would have seemed almost inconceivable in a 'normal' year, where the usual issues were in contest. The Republicans could have run any 'traditional' candidates for the school board, and would not have been completely shut out. The rational, pragmatic residents of Guilford (i.e. almost all residents) would have considered any qualified candidates who weren't pitching wild unproven conspiracy theories.

But the five candidates that prevailed in the Republican Town Committee caucus—and then immediately appeared on *Fox & Friends* to spread the word—were playing a national game that didn't sell in the heart of New England. Or stated more colorfully: 'that dog won't hunt in Guilford.' The maneuver had merely served to turn off most residents (and terrify many), driving voters of all stripes to the polls in record numbers. No Republicans were elected to the Board of Education because the CRT conspiracy team didn't merely overreach. It did so in what felt like desperation.

CHAPTER FIFTEEN

TO A PERSON WITH A HAMMER...

Does this tale end like one of those 'feel good' stories, where the town all comes together after a bruising, contentious election, and everyone embraces the commendable objectives described in '*The Guilford Covenant*?' So far, that seems not to be the case. For one thing, before, during and after the election, there was grousing from the Row 'B' camp. Their attempted, conservative school board apotheosis had been stolen from them. They'd been swindled by what they perceived to be '*fraud*' in the manner in which voters of all stripes had pulled together to circumvent the 'minority representation' rule.

That rule was adopted to avoid one-party dominance. It was intended as a structural bulwark—a governor, to encourage a degree of bipartisan moderation. Over the years, the rule has benefitted each party when it was in the minority. But the 2021 election raised a previously not-contemplated conundrum: what's a town to do when the 'minority party' candidates are running on a culture war platform that is completely toxic to most of the voters? The outcome of the 2021 BOE election—with two Democrats and three Independents resoundingly defeating all five GOP candidates—seemed to rather firmly answer that nettlesome question. One would have thought (at least, I'd hoped) that a lesson might have been learned. *Surely the culture warriors will reassess their strategy going forward…right?*

Wrong!

I had clearly gotten too comfortable applauding the outcome of the 2021 Guilford BOE election. Just days after the election results should have put an end to their conspiracy accusations, the Row 'B' crowd was back. On November 11, 2021 an article appeared in the *Guilford Courier* that was headlined: '***Voters Overwhelmingly Reject GOP BOE***

Candidates.' In that article, one of the losing candidates (Bill Maisano) described the election results as *"actually tremendous for us. This is actually big for us…"*

Mr. Maisano promised that henceforth a lot of *"eyes are going to be watching this superintendent and every single thing that goes on in that school."* He was presumably referring to the eyes of 1-out-of-3 voters who hadn't flat-out rebelled against his CRT conspiracy theory. In a December 16, 2021 *Guilford Courier* article, another candidate (Danielle Scarpellino) had reportedly claimed that she and the other Republicans had scored a *'major victory.'*

Ummmm…if this was what the Republican candidates considered a *'major victory,'* then a quick historical note to the pyrrhic victors could be in order. There are almost always 30-some percent of voters who will vote for *any* candidate, and support *any* cause (no matter how repugnant it may be to the majority). Even Joe McCarthy—the Godfather of government conspiracy theories—retained a faithful phalanx of supporters. When a politician's approval ratings are in the 30% range? It's time to look for another windmill at which to tilt.

Anyway, those responses of the Row 'B' team to the outcome of the election were not exactly decorous concessions to the mandate of an overwhelming majority of Guilford's voters. More like mystifying displays of hubris. Alas, such are the times in which we live. This shouldn't have surprised me, yet somehow it did. For some reason I had in my head a quaint, old-fashioned notion, that candidates could still display humility and grace in defeat—especially when the defeat had been 'historic' (and in Guilford, that's *really* saying something).

Rather than that, the losers have informed us that they have won some sort of major victory. A Potemkin village of alleged support for their CRT conspiracy has been erected before the dubious eyes of the town. In historic Guilford, the days of humility in defeat are apparently history as well. In the current political climate, claiming victory in defeat has become *de rigueur.* Evidently even Guilford is not immune to that trend. I suppose we can at least be thankful that the losers hadn't requested a recount of their landslide defeat, and then demanded the seizure of voting machines. But I wondered: *did those bellicose statements from the candidates simply represent a reflexive difficulty in acknowledging defeat? Or were they harbingers of more whacky maneuvering to come?*

By early spring of 2022, I started to seriously put pen to paper. Fortunately, the Independent 'heroes' of the 2021 election were *way ahead of me.* They had already recognized something with which I was just beginning to come to grips. They saw more than the story that I was contemplating, about disaster narrowly averted. This wasn't a one-off. They saw an *ongoing threat* to the ideals of '*The Guilford Covenant.*' They'd seen that the horses were out of the barn—and apparently enjoying their wild ride in the sun too much to stop anytime soon. In early January 2022, Independent voters caucused to create a new political party, Independent Guilford (IG). They hadn't just written about it. As in 2021, they had actually done something about it. Thanks to them, a bulwark had been put in place, to counter any future crazy stuff (coming from *either* of the other two parties in town). Which was a very good thing for Guilford…because…

Just four months after her candidates had been thrashed at the polls, Mary Beeman was back, and sharing anew with the readers of the *Guilford Courier* her theory that Marxism was still careening through the hallways of our schools. I thought: *please tell me you're not laying the groundwork for a 2023 campaign—and doing it by trotting out the exact same failed argument?* She became especially fretful about certain words and phrases that triggered in her sinister suspicions. The word '*work*' [that teachers were doing in our schools] *really* got her going in a March 10, 2022 '*Letter to the Editor.*'

"'The *work*,'" she pondered suspiciously, "what is it and how is it manifested…?" She narrated from the CRT conspiracy playbook, rambling on about oppressors and oppressed and such. She encouraged every parent to question their kids every day, to find out what was really going on in those menacing classrooms. I thought: *They just lost the election by a mile—yet they're still pitching the same stuff.* My thoughts began to crystallize into a certain realization: *These folks may not have been stirring up racial animus as a purely political tactic to gain power. They might actually believe this conspiracy business.*

That notion was, in a sense, oddly comforting (in that they might be motivated more by atavistic instinct than cynical calculation). All the same, it was also worrisome if they actually believed that the Guilford Public School System—among the best in the country—was riddled with Marxist anti-White racist conspirators.

It has been suggested that, to a person with a hammer, every problem can resemble a nail. Apparently to socially conservative Christian conspiracy theorists armed with a national right-wing playbook (and out-of-town money), seemingly benign everyday words and names can conjure terrifying Marxist conspiracies. A very recent case illustrates that point fairly clearly. In a February 2, 2023 *Guilford Courier* 'Letter to the Editor,' one of the town's most conspicuous conspiracy propagandists (Dave Holman) busted out nearly every one of the classic CRT conspiracy tropes. He took dead aim at a suspicious local club that is apparently a thinly veiled front for nefarious Marxist activities (and they're up to their shenanigans right under our noses, in the Guilford Public Library).

Soon enough, I found myself drafting a response.

Finally! Someone with gumption to reveal the scariest conspiracy yet. Mass shootings? Climate change? Assaults on democracy? Constitutional rights abridged? Putin flattening Ukraine? Hey, things happen. Niggling matters shouldn't distract from important stuff.

Big shout-out to Dave Holman. Last month he exposed the transgender kids support boondoggle (Jan. 12 "Is This How We Want ARPA Funds Spent?"). Now he's pulled back the curtain on 'The Big Hearts Book Club!' (Feb. 23, "Troubling"). Gotta admit, they had me fooled. Then again, I'm new to conspiracy-spotting. Here's rule #1: If the name makes you smile? It's a Marxist cell. A word sounds benign? Marxist "code-speak." Salutary cause? Marxist plot. Thankfully the "Oh-Say-Can-You-See-The-Conspiracy Club" is ever-poised to expose sinister capers like Marxist mommies indoctrinating 6-year-olds. While I naïvely smiled at their name, veteran spotters consulted the "Conspiracy Cipher Guidebook." Holman warns: Don't be hoodwinked by "social-emotional storytime" or "caring, empathetic kids."

"The problem," he explains, "is that social-emotional learning (SEL) is code speak for Critical Race Theory (CRT) indoctrination, otherwise known as culturally responsive education, diversity-equity-inclusion, critical thinking, antiracism, Marxism, and equity and social justice."

Drat. I'd forgotten rule #2 (rookie mistake): Marxist code-speak is super-efficient. SEL includes every unsavory plot. Holman says there's something "even worse." Get this: apparently 'Big Hearted' parents are using "the same raised hands logo that appears on lawn signs all over Guilford in support of...'Equity and Social Justice Initiative.'" Gasp! That's bad. Also confusing. Why would those signs of support be "all over Guilford?"

Holman asks: "[I]s this how our tax dollars should be spent?" How about 'The Big Grinch Book Club' instead? We could turn cute little kids (CLK) into insensitive uncaring adults (IUA) who wouldn't waste money on fluffy conceits like empathy and tolerance.

—Greg Kinsella
  Guilford, CT

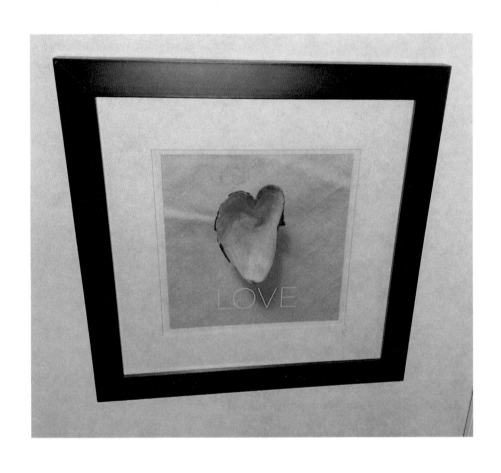

CHAPTER SIXTEEN

PARALLEL UNIVERSES

The point is that after getting clobbered at the polls, the usual right-wing conspiracy theorists in town remain unchastened and voluble, forcing their culture war leitmotif upon conflict-weary residents who mostly don't care to hear it. I now refuse to fall back into my old '*tune-out*' default mode. I tolerate as much of the silly stuff as I can, for as long as I can. When my blood pressure reaches a certain point, I feel compelled to offer up my 'alternative' viewpoint. (I'm pretty sure sarcasm is justifiable if it's purely medicinal)

For some of my opinions, I've drawn metaphorical return fire from the pen of one of the *Guilford Courier's* most bombastic right-wing letter-writers (and leading CRT conspiracy theorist): Kendall Svengalis (aficionados of 19th century European literature might find a certain irony in that surname). Last spring, he described me as living in a 'parallel universe.' I completely agree with that proposition, given the ideological space wherein the conspiracy theorists appear to reside.

In that May 5, 2022 *Guilford Courier* 'Letter to the Editor,' Mr. Svengalis unleashed a fusillade of unsavory adjectives to describe me, and my agenda as he divined it to be. Apparently I'd been guilty of the sin of "*obfuscation.*" I'm thinking that must have been because I had quoted Mary Beeman's *actual words*, as opposed to accepting the omniscient '*Svengalis explanation*' of "*what Mary meant*" when she'd uttered those precise 18 words?

Mr. Svengalis concluded that I was "*uninformed,*" and "*mean-spirited.*" As to my direct challenge to the relentless assaults against our educators? He deemed that to have been "*an unwarranted and dishonest hate fest.*" I was said to belong to a disagreeable contingent within the community "*who have no sense of decency, and seek to take words out of context to serve…radical political ends.*"

Geez! I did all that?

Mr. Svengalis concluded that I was in '*denial*' and '*confused.*' Since admittedly, I'm not yet fully on board with his theory that everyone in our school system is a lying racist Marxist conspirator, I suppose in his conspiracy universe (or at least his CRT galaxy), that would tend to make me appear confused.

Mr. Svengalis also determined that others and I had been feebly attempting "*to distract*" from "*Superintendent of Schools Dr. Paul Freeman's incompetent leadership.*" Wait…Paul Freeman? If that name sounds a bit familiar, it is because that would be the exact same Dr. Freeman who was the 2021 Connecticut Superintendent of the Year. I think all would agree that my universe employs a somewhat different definition of the word 'competence.'

The conspiracy universe is vast. Within it lies the CRT conspiracy galaxy, which relies upon a familiar brand of right wing alchemy (along with a healthy dose of artifice) to transform black into white, and white into black. It starts with sinister suspicions and strident recriminations. The same voices regurgitate and amplify accusations at a frenetic cadence and deafening volume. It usually requires the suspension of all skepticism about claims that don't sound quite right.

Since the CRT conspiracy galaxy has a website, replete with its own lexicon, it can clarify all the things that don't otherwise seem to add up. For instance, in the CRT conspiracy galaxy, being 'anti' something doesn't mean you're *against* it. It actually means you're *FOR* it. '*Anti-racism*' is really Marxist code for '*racism against White people.*' If we choose to support 'equity and social justice,' we are in fact acting *inequitably and unjustly.* It seems complicated, but it's really all quite simple, if we just listen to the folks behind the curtain, and remember the time-tested lessons of our youth, when everyone played a certain game: "*I know you are…but what am I?*"

Those residing in the CRT conspiracy galaxy have fashioned a theory that would have us believe that our teachers and administrators have been indoctrinating students with Marxist ideology. Ibram Kendi's actual "*goal,*" Mr. Svengalis explained pedantically, is "*racial revenge.*" He warned in his May 5 letter that "[t]hese views, and the radical pedagogy that flows from it *[sic]*, have no place in our schools."

Hmmmm. I think I'm beginning to achieve a tenuous grasp of how this big conspiracy puzzle fits together. In the CRT conspiracy galaxy, the theory seems to go something like this: In the mostly White Town of Guilford…the White Superintendent of Schools… and the mostly White teachers, administrators and Board of Education members…are all furtively conspiring to inculcate our mostly White students with sinister Marxist ideology…which is harmful…to White kids.

Why, one might wonder, would all those people be doing such things? Although I admit, that question has puzzled me, apparently things are clear to the cognoscenti behind the curtain. The implication seems to be that everyone under the thrall of Dr. Freeman must be striving to achieve Kendi's and their shared goal…of exacting *'racial revenge'*…against *White people.* Because…ummm…even though they're mostly White…ummm…they're…like…*racist against Whites…because they're Marxists?* I mean—they've been *'re-educated?'* Or something to do with a *'lens of Marxism?'*

To me, it all sounds a bit preposterous. Then again, I'm not yet fully fluent in Marxist idioms. Could it be that the CRT conspiracy galaxy is on an eventual collision course with the Q-Anon galaxy? Or perhaps even the Pizza-Gate galaxy? Its residents are definitely correct about one thing: I *am* pretty darn confused. It turns out I really stink at figuring out byzantine race-based Marxist conspiracies. And admitting to possess no 'personal knowledge' as to what goes on these days within our Guilford School District or Board of Education, I concede that I may be dead wrong. I suppose the complicated conspiracy theory might be true? Perhaps I am 'in denial' in my parallel universe?' Presumably time will tell. Still, until that particular conspiracy theory is proven true, I'll soldier on with my guileless trust that Guilford's educators, administrators, and *unpaid* BOE members (yes, despite all the slings and arrows they've had to suffer, they are *UNPAID*), will continue to do exactly what they've done throughout all our decades in Guilford.

In other words, I'll stick to my parallel universe, which seems so much simpler. It also benefits from the immutable laws of geometry (in my universe, things such as math and science are not evil conspiracies), which assure that our parallel paths will never meet. That's okay with me. Still though, our universes seem to be close enough that we can call each other names, and then talk past each other. We sure don't seem to be convincing each other of much. Frankly, in the overall scheme of things, it all just seems rather silly.

CHAPTER SEVENTEEN

DEFENDING 'THE COVENANT' (AS AMENDED)

It occurs to me that the next generation of kids going through the Guilford Public Schools will have a lot of things to figure out and address—much of which will have been caused and/or ignored by the generations preceding them. Our planet is roasting. Fifty-year weather events are happening every year. Some states and countries are on fire, as reservoirs dry up; while others are under water. At times, the mighty Mississippi looks more like mud pie than a river. Meanwhile, across the globe, Putin seems hell-bent on obliterating the sovereign nation of Ukraine, causing millions to be displaced, maimed or killed.

In America, democracy and voting rights and other civil rights are under assault. Personal 'Constitutional rights'—such as those that had been codified 50 years ago by Roe v. Wade—have been exterminated with the firm gavel-rap of a Supreme Court that seems determined to turn the nation into a theocracy. Hate crimes proliferate against people because of their skin color or sexual orientation or ethnicity or religion. Guns are everywhere; mass shootings a regular occurrence (including in schools and places of worship). And despite the hopeful aspirations alluded to by Dr. King over half a century ago, it would be a serious stretch to suggest that all people in this country are now judged solely by the content of their character.

Yup! Today's Guilford students will eventually branch out and forge paths into a fraught world—one that likely will be much more diverse than Guilford, Connecticut. They will certainly have plenty of messes to clean up; messes not of their making but caused or tolerated by generations of feckless 'adults' that preceded them. Despite all that, the most pressing issue to the local White Christian conservative chapter of CRT conspiracy galaxy, seems to be the curious matter of what books teachers have read? They haven't yet proposed banning teachers from reading 'certain' books. But can that tactic be far away?

The conspiracy theory practitioners don't like me very much for being such a skeptic. And fortunately, none of that personal stuff matters in the least. Because as long as most of Guilford continues to support, and vote for empathy and tolerance, I can handle some sharp elbows in the corners from a few obdurate hecklers (I played hockey a lifetime ago). One thing's for sure though: it's gonna feel like an eternity before the next BOE election rolls around in November—especially given recent, roiling developments on our public education front. On September 1, 2022—less than 10 months after the 'historic' BOE election results—the Guilford Courier's front-page trumpeted this headline: *'Parents Threaten Lawsuit Over CRT Claims.'*

Well of course. That's democracy in action. Lose huge at the polls; then bring a lawsuit to get the result that the historic majority of voters had just rejected. The Row 'B' candidates have hired an attorney, with a stated goal to "lead to an overhaul of the BOE and force the resignation of current School Superintendent Dr. Paul Freeman." The *Guilford Courier* article didn't quote any of the plaintiffs reflecting upon Guilford's impressive public school rankings; or the prestigious award that had been bestowed in 2021 upon Dr. Freeman. The article did quote Bill Maisano, who described the Guilford Board of Education as "lazy…" (which may be a technical legal term).

Okay then…

Some of the Row 'B' plaintiffs have hired Attorney Norman Pattis to represent them. He's well known in these parts, most notably of late for defending the nation's preeminent conspiracy theorist, Alex Jones, in a defamation lawsuit brought by the families of some of those killed in the Sandy Hook school shooting. A verdict of nearly *one billion dollars* in compensatory damages was recently awarded by the jury in that case, and then augmented by nearly *half-billion dollars* in punitive damages. Attorney Pattis' law license in Connecticut was ordered suspended for 6 months by the judge in that case, but that order is being appealed. One way or another, he should be back in the fold in plenty of time to prosecute the Row 'B' litigation.

Further reporting suggests that those Row 'B' plaintiffs have not solely alleged dissatisfaction with their interpretation of the GPS 'curriculum' (i.e. the CRT conspiracy theory). They have also asserted in their complaint that certain teachers and administrators have subjected the plaintiffs' children to *'punishment'* because they (the parents) had been *"critics of the board."*

That, of course, would be an entirely different kettle of fish. If proven true, that would be unacceptable conduct. Those allegations have been made in court filings, and vigorously denied by the defendants. It may take a while, but eventually (remember—the wheels of justice turn slowly), those factual disputes should be resolved in court. Whether the United States District Court will exercise its '*federal court jurisdiction*' to analyze and direct 'state educational guidelines,' and the Town of Guilford's compliance with them, remains to be seen.

I won't pretend to know a single thing about contested factual claims, involving children allegedly being 'punished' in school. But I have no doubt at all that the lives of the kids of the Row 'B' plaintiffs must be difficult. By now, most kids in town have undoubtedly heard rumors—if not actually followed the reporting—about how the parents of a handful of their schoolmates have accused Guilford's teachers and school administrators of being lying racist Marxist conspirators.

The drumbeat of those allegations has continued for over 2 years. It continues to this day, notwithstanding the Election Day repudiation of those claims by the voters. Kids of a certain age (say adolescence) can be pretty darn rough. As those Row 'B' parents continue to level the same charges against Guilford's teachers and administrators, the '*Row B children*' have undoubtedly been thrust, time-and-again, into some exceedingly difficult situations with their peers. That is beyond sad for those kids.

To add additional intrigue to the enduring saga, a *Guilford Courier* story on September 15, 2022, revealed what may be a fitting coda to the CRT conspiracy saga. Apparently, some outfit based in Idaho is providing financial assistance to the Row 'B' plaintiffs in support of their lawsuit. That organization has a catchy name: '*We The Patriots, USA.*' It was described as a 'non-profit' in the *Guilford Courier*. It has a self-described goal [to] "*create a powerful network of Patriots to preserve and reclaim our God-given inalienable rights.*" That rather ambitious *raison d'etre* raises a question or two.

If a bunch of local voters—let's just randomly say 2 out of every 3 of us—oppose an Idaho outfit pushing a lawsuit against Guilford's Board of Education, its teachers, and its Superintendent of the Year—would that automatically make us unpatriotic? If so, could we resolve that infraction, by creating our own non-profit…maybe with an even more patriotic-sounding name? Would something like '*We The Super-Patriotic Majority of Voters of Guilford, Connecticut, USA, Milky Way Galaxy,*' get us back into the good graces of whoever gives out patriotism ribbons? Would it be unpatriotic for people to look at distracting stuff like…I dunno…'*school systems*'…before deciding whether we want some Idaho outfit financing a lawsuit that the Town of Guilford will have to spend money to defend? Because I gotta say, if out-of-staters get to have a hand in spending our money, and running our schools? For my two cents, I'd rather have Massachusetts's folks running the show for us.

According to the '*World Population Review*' (2022) rankings of public school systems, Connecticut schools rank *second in the country*—behind only Massachusetts. The 2023 Connecticut State Department of Education (CSDE) rankings have the Guilford Public School System (K-12), ranked #5 in the state. Incidentally, for what it's worth, Idaho public schools are stuck around the bottom third of the country, ranked at #34 (I'm just sayin'…). Maybe '*We The Patriots, USA*' should consider spreading more of its patriotic cash around its own state? Or does it believe that every town has a God-given inalienable right to a school system that ranks in the low to middling range? All the same, I have a sneaky feeling the taxpayers of Guilford would prefer to stick with one of the best school systems in the country, and the Board of Education and Superintendent that they overwhelmingly supported with their votes in 2021.

According to *Guilford Courier* reporting, '*We The Patriots, USA*' is funding other, similar lawsuits, across the country. I guess that means Marxism must be careening into the classrooms of secondary schools all across America? To think—if only we'd listened to the culture warriors in 2021, we wouldn't be in this pickle today. If voters hadn't widely rejected those five conspiracy candidates, *they* would be running the show. By now, Guilford could be well on its way to achieving a school system just as patriotic as Idaho's (where I'm guessing White Christian conservative kids probably feel like they *really* belong).

The September 1, 2022 *Guilford Courier* article mentioned that the losing BOE candidates (i.e. the plaintiffs) claim to have 'evidence' that Guilford schools are teaching Critical Race Theory. It seems it would have been more efficient to publish that evidence for the voters to assess *before* the 2021 election. But hey, as the saying goes: the world needs more expensive lawsuits. I just hope the cost of defending that Row 'B' lawsuit won't increase taxes on Guilford residents. We know how taxes can be a sensitive topic for *some* residents. In fact, even *I* might get rankled by that.

Heck, am I becoming a fiscal conservative in my old age?

So what is the point of this ramble? The point is that the 2021 electoral rebuke of the 'socially conservative' conspiracy theorists did not end their crusade in Guilford. It continues undeterred, its practitioners preaching the same dogma, with near-religious fervor. And for anyone who thinks this sort of thing couldn't happen in his or her town? Think again.

In 1639, the settlers of Guilford conceived a foundational principle, as set forth in '*The Guilford Covenant*': Mutual cooperation and assistance among Guilford's residents would inure to the benefit of each individually, and all collectively. For nearly 4 centuries, residents have remained dedicated to living out that worthy conception. And yet, even in Guilford, shadows have now been cast upon our venerated 'Covenant.' Ideological divisions have alarmed most residents. If that has happened, and is *still* happening, in Guilford, Connecticut…it could literally happen in any town.

In trying times, I often find comfort in the immortal words of our greatest President (who was a 30 year-old Illinois State Representative, when Guilford celebrated its 200th birthday). To *re-phrase* what may have been Lincoln's most important 271 words: Now we are engaged in an ideological civil war, testing whether that town, or any town, so conceived, and so dedicated, can remain true to its foundational 'Covenant.' The answer thus far seems to be: '*that depends.*'

We are probably long overdue for a contemporary 'amendment' to '*The Guilford Covenant*' (it's approaching 4 centuries old…it's had a nice run). The U.S. Constitution has had dozens of amendments. In a town of over 20,000 residents, it's unrealistic to expect that *everyone* will always work together. But when it comes to the really important stuff, we can decide what kind of town we want to be. In November 2021, a historic majority of Guilford's voters decisively answered that question at the polls. As long as we remain engaged, and willing to work together—with votes, words, and actions—we can do it again. We can defend 'The Covenant' (as amended)—if we clearly and resolutely oppose intolerance, however and whenever it rears its noxious head.

THE END